Tl... ...
OF THE HUMAN BODY

Physical Regeneration According to
the Laws of Chemistry and Physiology.

&

THE CHEMISTRY OF HUMAN LIFE

The Biochemic Statement of the Cause of Disease and the
Physiological and Chemical Operation of the Inorganic Salts
of the Human Organism and their Chemical Formulas

&

THE TREE OF LIFE

An Expose of Physical Regenesis on the Three-fold Plane of
Bodily, Chemical and Spiritual Operation.

BY GEORGE W. CAREY

CONTENT

THE WONDERS
OF THE HUMAN BODY

Physical Regeneration According to
the Laws of Chemistry and Physiology.

BY GEORGE W. CAREY

FOREWORD

June 1st, 1917, Dr. Carey published the Tree of Life, a book on the marvels of the human body and physical regeneration as taught in Greek and Hebrew texts, from which the English Bible was translated.

The book aroused such intense interest that the edition was virtually sold out in less than a year.

The Wonders of the Human Body may be termed "an enlarged edition of the Tree of Life", containing more than double the amount of information.

Many more Bible witnesses have been called to the stand, than were heard in the Tree of Life, to testify to the truths of Scripture and to indubitably prove that the Greek and Hebrew writings were based in the truths of chemistry and physiology.

This book was not compiled for the purpose of antagonizing so-called Christians. It was written to prove the truths of the fables, parables and splendid allegories, such as the book of Job and Revelations, with a firm faith that truth will triumph and at last lead the world to Peace.

THE AUTHOR

Los Angeles, California, September 7, 1918.

PART ONE

THE WONDERS
OF THE HUMAN BODY

"For thou didst cover me in my mother's womb.
I will give thanks unto thee; for I am fearfully
and wonderfully made;
Wonderful are thy works."

—139th Ps., 13 and 14-th v.

The human race has been asleep, and has dreamed that property and money are the true wealth of a nation, sacrificing men, women and children to the chimerical idea that danced in visionary splendor through their brains. The result of this is to be seen in the uneasiness that prevails everywhere. But humanity is waking up, slowly but surely, and beginning to realize that it, itself, is the most precious thing on earth.

The old-established statement that the individuals that make up the race are imperfect is no more true than that a pile of lumber is imperfect, that is to be afterward reformed, or built into a house. As it is the carpenter's business to take the lumber, which is perfect as material, and build the house, so it is the legitimate work of spiritual man to take the perfect material everywhere present and build, by the perfect law of chemistry and mathematics, the perfected, harmonious human being, and, with this material, employ the same law to build up society collectively.

It is a well-known physiological fact that the blood is the basic material of which the human body is continually builded. As is the blood, so is the body; as is the body, so is the brain; as is the brain, so is the quality of thought. As a man is builded, so thinks he.

According to the views of students of modern alchemy, the Bible—both the Old and the New Testaments—are symbolical writings, based primarily upon this very process of body building. The word alchemy really means fleshology. It is derived from chem, an ancient Egyptian word, meaning flesh. The word Egypt also means flesh, or anatomy.

Alchemy, however, in its broader scope, means the science of solar rays. Gold may be traced to the sun's rays. The word gold means solar essence. The transmutation of gold does not mean the process of making gold, but does mean the process of changing gold, solar rays, into all manner of materialized forms, vegetable, mineral, etc. The ancient alchemist studied the process of Nature in her operations from the volatile to the fixed, the fluid to the solid, the essence to the substance, or the abstract to the concrete, all of which may be summed up in the changing of spirit into matter. In reality, the alchemist did not try to do anything. He simply tried to search out nature's processes in order that he might comprehend her marvelous operations.

To be sure, language was used that to us seems symbolical and often contradictory, but it was not so intended, nor so at all in reality. We speak in symbols. If a man is in delirium, caused by alcohol in his brain-cells, we say he has "snakes in his boots." Of course, no one supposes that the words are to be taken literally. Yet, if our civilization should be wiped out, and our literature translated after four or five thousand years, those who read our history might be puzzled to know what was meant by "snakes in his boots."

Again, it has been believed by most people that the words, "transmutation of base metals into gold," used by alchemists, referred to making gold. But a careful study of the Hebrew Cosmogony, and the Kabala, will reveal the fact that the alchemist always referred to solar rays when he used the word gold. By "base metals," they simply meant matter, or basic material. The dissolving or disintegration of matter, the combustion of wood or coal, seemed as wonderful to these philosophers as the growth of wood or the formation of coal or stone. So the transmutation of base metals into gold simply meant the process of changing the fixed into the volatile, or the dematerialization of matter, either by heat or chemical process.

It is believed by modern students of alchemy that the books of the Old and New Testaments are a collection of alchemical and astrological writings, dealing entirely with the wonderful operation of aerial elements (spirit) in the human body, so fearfully and wonderfully made. The same authority is given for the statement, "Know ye not that your bodies are the temple of the living God" and "Come unto Me all ye that labor and are heavy laden and I will give you rest." According to the method of reading the numerical value of letters by the Kabala, M and E figure B, when united. Our B is from the Hebrew Beth, meaning a house or temple—the temple of the spiritual ego—the body. Thus by coming into the realization that the body is really the Father's House, temple of God, the spirit secures peace and contentment or rest.

The human body is composed of perfect principles, gases, minerals, molecules, or atoms; but these builders of flesh and bone are not always properly adjusted. The planks or bricks used in building houses may be endlessly diversified in arrangement, and yet be perfect material.

Solomon's temple is an allegory of man's temple the human organism. This house is built (always being built) "without sound of saw or hammer."

The real Ego manifests in a house, beth, church, or temple— i. e., Soul-of-Man's Temple, for the Ego or I AM.

The solar (soular) plexus is the great central sun or dynamo on which the Subconscious Mind (another name for God) operates and causes the concept of individual consciousness. Specifically stated thus :

1. The upper brain (cerebrum) ; "The Most High" or Universal Father, which furnishes substance for all functions that constitute the body.

2. The Spiritual Ego ("I AM") resident in the cerebellum.

3. The Son of God, the redeeming seed or Jesus, born monthly in the solar plexus.

4. Soul, the fluids of the body.

5. Flesh, bone, etc., the fluids materialized. (In a broader sense body also is termed soul, "Every soul perished.") It is not thinkable that every Spirit, or Ego or "I AM" was drowned.

No wonder that the seers and alchemists of old declared that "Your bodies are the temple of the living God" and "The kingdom of Heaven is within you." But man, blinded by selfishness, searches here and there, scours the heavens with his telescope, digs deep into earth, and dives into ocean's depths, in a vain search for the elixir of life that may be found between the soles of his feet and the crown of his head. Really our human body is a miracle of mechanism. No work of man can compare with it in accuracy of its process and the simplicity of its laws.

At maturity, the human skeleton contains about 165 bones, so delicately and perfectly adjusted that science has despaired of ever imitating it. The muscles are about 500 in number; length of alimentary canal, 32 feet; amount of blood in average adult, 30 pounds, or one-fifth the weight of the body; the heart is six inches in length and four inches in diameter, and beats seventy times per minute, 4200 times per hour, 100,800 per day, 36,720,000 per year. At each beat, two and one-half ounces of blood are thrown out of it, 175 ounces per minute, 656 pounds per hour, or about eight tons per day.

All the blood in the body passes through the heart every three minutes; and during seventy years it lifts 270,000,000 tons of blood.

The lungs contain about one gallon of air at their usual degree of inflation. We breathe, on an average, 1200 breaths per hour; inhale 600 gallons of air, or 24,000 gallons daily.

The aggregate surface of the air-cells of the lungs exceeds 20,000 square inches, an area nearly equal to that of a room twelve feet square. The average weight of the brain of an adult is three pounds, eight ounces; the average female brain, two pounds, four ounces. The convolutions of a woman's brain cells and tissues are finer and more delicate in fibre and mechanism, which evidently accounts for the intuition of women. It would appear that the difference in the convolutions and fineness of tissue in brain matter is responsible for the degrees of consciousness called reason and intuition.

The nerves are all connected with the brain directly, or by the spinal marrow, but nerves receive their sustenance from the blood, and their motive power from the solar plexus dynamo.

The nerves, together with the branches and minute ramifications, probably exceed ten millions in number, forming a bodyguard outnumbering the mightiest army ever marshalled.

The skin is composed of three layers, and varies from one-eighth to one-quarter of an inch in thickness. The average area of skin is estimated to be about 2000 square inches. The atmospheric pressure, being fourteen pounds to the square inch, a person of medium size is subject to a pressure of 40,000 pounds. Each square inch of skin contains 3500 sweat tubes, or perspiratory pores (each of which may be likened to a little drain tile) one-fourth of an inch in length, making an aggregate length of the entire surface of the body of 201,166 feet, or a tile for draining the body nearly forty miles in length.

Our body takes in an average of five and a half pounds of food and drink each day, which amounts to one ton of solid and liquid nourishment annually, so that in seventy years a man eats and drinks 1000 times his own weight.

There is not known in all the realms of architecture or mechanics one little device which is not found in the human organism. The pulley, the lever, the inclined plane, the hinge, the "universal joint," tubes and trap-doors; the scissors, grind-stone, whip, arch, girders, filters, valves, bellows, pump, camera, and Aeolian harp; and irrigation plant, telegraph and telephone systems all these and a hundred other devices which man thinks he has invented, but which have only been telegraphed to the brain from the Solar Plexus (cosmic centre) and crudely copied or manifested on the objective canvas.

No arch ever made by man is as perfect as the arch formed by the upper ends of the two legs and the pelvis to support the weight of the trunk. No palace or cathedral ever built has been provided with such a perfect system of arches and girders.

No waterway on earth is so complete, so commodious, or so populous as that wonderful river of life, the "Stream of Blood." The violin, the trumpet, the harp, the grand organ, and all the other musical instruments, are mere counterfeits of the human voice.

Man has tried in vain to duplicate the hinges of the knee, elbow, fingers and toes, although they are a part of his own body.

Another marvel of the human body is the self-regulation process by which nature keeps the temperature in health at 98 degrees. Whether in India, with the temperature at 130 degrees, or in the arctic regions, where the records show 120 degrees below the freezing point, the temperature of the body remains the same, practically steady at 98 degrees, despite the extreme to which it is subjected.

It was said that "All roads lead to Rome." Modern science has discovered that all roads of real knowledge lead to the human body. The human body is an epitome of the universe; and when man turns within the mighty searchings of reason and investigation that he has so long used without—the "New Heaven and Earth" will appear.

While it is true that flesh is made by a precipitation of blood, it is not true that blood is made from food. The inorganic or cell-salts contained in food are set free by the process of combustion or digestion, and carried into the circulation through the delicate absorbent tubes of the mucous membrane of stomach and intestines. Air, or Spirit, breathed into the lungs, enters the arteries (air carriers) and chemically unites with the mineral base, and by a wonderful transformation creates flesh, bone, hair, nails, and all the fluids of the body.

On the rock (Peter or Petra, meaning stone) of the mineral salts is the human structure built, and the grave, stomach, or hell shall not prevail against it. The minerals in the body do not disintegrate or rot in the grave.

The fats, albumen, fibrine, etc., that compose the organic part of food, are burned up in the process of digestion and transposed into energy or force to run the human battery. Blood is made from air; thus all nations that dwell on earth are of one blood, for all breathe one air. The best food is the food that burns up quickest and easiest; that is, with the least friction in the human furnace.

The sexual functions of man and woman; the holy operation of creative energy manifested in male and female; the formation of life germs in ovum and sex fluids; the Divine Procedure of the "word made flesh" and the mysteries of conception and birth are the despair of science.

"Know ye not that your bodies are the temple of the living God?" for "God breathed into man the breath of life."

In the words of Epictitus, "Unhappy man, thou bearest a god with thee, and knoweth it not."

Walt Whitman sings:

"I loaf and invite my soul; I lean and loaf at my ease, observing a spear of summer grass. Clean and sweet is my soul, and clean and sweet is all that is not my soul."

"Welcome every organ and attribute of me, and of any man hearty and clean, not an inch, not a particle of an inch, is vile, and none shall be less familiar than the rest."

"Divine am I, inside and out, and I make holy whatever I touch or am touched from."

"I say no man has ever yet been half devout enough; none has ever yet adored or worshipped half enough; none has begun to think how divine he himself is, and how certain the future is."

The vagus nerve, so named because of its wandering (vagrant) branches, is the greatest marvel of the human organism. Grief depresses the circulation through the vagus, a condition of malnutrition follows, and tuberculosis, often of the hasty type, follows.

The roots of the vagus nerve are in the medulla oblongata, at the base of the small brain or cerebellum, and explains why death follows the severing of the medulla. It controls the heart action, and if a drug such as aconite be administered, even in small doses, its effect upon this nerve is shown in slowing the action of the heart and decreasing the blood pressure. In larger doses it paralyzes the ends of the vagus in the heart, so that the pulse becomes suddenly very rapid and at the same time irregular. Branches of the vagus nerve reach the heart, lungs, stomach, liver and kidneys.

Worry brings on kidney disease, but it is the vagus nerve, and especially that branch running to the kidneys which undue excitement or worry, or strain, brings about the paralysis of the kidneys in the performance of their functions.

When we say that a man's heart sinks within him from fear or apprehension, it is shown by the effect of this nerve up on the heart action. If his heart beats high with hopes, or he sighs for relief, it is the vagus nerve that has conducted the mental state to the heart and accelerated its action or caused that spasmodic action of the lungs which we call a sigh.

The nerves of the human body constitute the "Tree of Life," with its leaves of healing. The flowing waters of the "Rivers of Life" are the veins and arteries through which sweep the red, magnetic currents of Love of Spirit made visible.

Behold the divine telegraph system, the million nerve wires running throughout the wondrous temple, the temple not made with hands, the temple made "without sound of saw or hammer." View the Central Sun of the human system—the Solar Plexus—vibrating life abundantly.

Around this dynamo of God, you may see the Beasts that worship before the Throne day and night saying, "Holy holy, art Thou, Lord God Almighty." The Beasts are the twelve plexuses of nerve centers, telegraph stations, like unto the twelve zodiacal signs that join hands in a fraternal circle across the gulf of space.

Aviation, liquified air, deep breathing for physical development and the healing of divers diseases rule the day. In every brain there are dormant cells, waiting for the "coming" of the bridegroom, the vibration of the air age (the Christ) that will resurrect them.

Everywhere we have evidence of the awakening of dormant brain cells. Much, if not all, of spiritual phenomena, multiple personality, mental telepathy, and kindred manifestations are explainable upon the hypothesis of the possibility of awakening and bringing into use of dormant brain cells.

Scientists have discovered that there are dormant, or undeveloped brain cells in countless number, especially in the cerebrum, or upper brain, the seat of the moral faculties; or, more definitely speaking, the key, which, when touched with the vital force set free through the process of physical regeneration by saving the seed and by the baptism in ointment (Christ) in the spinal cord, lifts the crucified substance wasted by the prodigal son in "riotous living" up to the "most high" brain.

This procedure causes the dormant cells, little buds, to actually bloom. The simile is perfect. The cells, while dormant, are like a flower yet in the bud. When the Substance that is needed for their development reaches them, through physical regeneration as outlined in the "Plan of Salvation," fully explained in part 2nd., the cells bloom and then vibrate at a rate that causes the Consciousness of the "New Birth." "He that is born of God doth not sin, for his seed remaineth in him." John.

The eye is hardly less wonderful, being a perfect photographer's camera. The retina is the dry plate on which are focused all objects by means of the crystalline lens. The cavity behind this lens is the shutter. The eyelid is the drop shuttle. The draping of the optical dark room is the only black membrane in the entire body. The miniature camera is self-focusing, self-loading and self-developing, and takes millions of pictures every day in colors and enlarged to life size. Charts have been prepared—marvelous charts—which go to show that the eye has 729 distinct expressions conveying as many distinct shades of meaning.

The power of color perception is overwhelming. To perceive red the retina of the eye must receive 395,000 vibrations in a second; for violet it must respond to 790,000,000. In our waking moments our eyes are bombarded every minute by at least 600,000,000 vibrations.

The ear contains a perfect miniature piano of about 3000 double fibers or strings stretched or relaxed in unison with exterior sounds. The longest cord of this marvelous instrument is one-fifteenth of an inch, while the shortest is about one-five-hundredth of an inch. The 3000 strings are distributed through a register of seven octaves, each octave corresponding to about 500 fibers and every half tone sub- divided again into 320 others. The deepest tone we can hear has thirty-two vibrations a second, the highest has 70,000.

The ear is a colossal mystery, and the phenomenon of sound is a secret only recorded in the Holy of Holies of the Infinite Mind. And what is mind? We know absolutely nothing about it. Some believe that mind is the product of the chemical operation of matter, viz. : the atoms or materials that compose the human body. These persons contend that all electrons are particles of pure Intelligence and KNOW what to do. Others hold to the theory that universal Mind (whatever it may be) forms a body from some material, they know not what, and then plays upon it or operates through it.

> Visions of beauty and splendor,
> Forms of a long-lost race,
> Sounds of voices and faces
> From the fourth dimensions of space;
> And on through the universe boundless,
> Our thoughts go, lightning-shod;
> Some call it Imagination,
> And others call it God!

Now comes speech, the Word that was in the beginning. God certainly bankrupted His infinite series of miracles when He gave the power of speech to man.

We wonder and adore in the presence of that pulsing orb, the heart. Tons of the water of life made red by the Chemistry of Love sweep through this central throne every day, and flow on to enrich the Edenic Garden until its waste places shall bloom and blossom as the rose.

Take my hand and go with me to the home of the Spiritual Ego—the wondrous brain. Can you count the whirling, electric, vibrating cells? No, not until you can count the sand grains on the ocean's shore. These rainbow-hued cells are the keys that the fingers of the soul strike to play its part in the Symphony of the Spheres.

At last we have seen the "Travail of the Soul and are satisfied." No more temples of the Magi now, but instead the glorious human Beth. At last we have found the true church of God, the human body. In this body, or church, spirit operates like some wizard chemist or electrician. No more searching through India's jungles or scaling the Himalayan heights in search for a master—a mahatma—or ancient priest, dwelling in some mysterious cave where occult rites and ceremonies are supposed to reveal the wisdom of the past. But, instead, you have found the Kingdom of the Real within the Temple that needs no outer Sun by day nor Moon or Stars by night to lighten it. And then the enraptured Soul becomes conscious that the stone has been rolled away from the door of material concept where it has slept, and it now hears the voice of the Father within saying, "Let there be light!" and feels the freedom that comes with knowing that Being is one.

And now man also realizes the meaning of the "Day of Judgment." He realizes that Judgment means understanding, hence the ability to judge. He then judges correctly, for he sees the Wisdom of Infinite Life in all men, in all things, all events, and all environments. Thus does the new birth take place, and the Kingdom of Harmony reigns now. Man must realize, however, that he is the creator or builder of his own body, and that he is responsible for every moment of its building, and every hour of its care. He alone can select and put together the materials provided by the universe for its construction. Man has been able to scale the heavens, to measure the distances between the stars and planetary bodies, and to analyze the component parts of suns and worlds, yet he cannot eat without making himself ill; he can foretell eclipses and tides for years in advance, but cannot look far enough ahead in his own affairs to say when he may be brought down with la grippe, or to calculate accurately the end of any bodily ill that may afflict him. When he finds out what he really is, and how much he has always had to do in the making of himself what he is, he will be ready to grasp some idea of the wonderful possibilities of every human body, and will know how completely and entirely is every man his own savior. Just so long as he denies his own powers, and looks outside of himself for salvation from present or future ills, he is indeed a lost creature. If the race is to be redeemed, it must come as the result of thought followed by action. If the race is to think differently than at present, it must have new bodies with new brains.

Modern physiologists know that our bodies are completely made over every year, by the throwing off of worn-out cells and the formation of new ones, that is going on every minute. Nature will take care of the making-over process, but we are responsible for the plan of reconstruction. Man must learn to run the machinery of his body with the same mathematical accuracy as he now displays in control of an engine or automobile, before he can lay claim to his divine heritage and proclaim himself master of his own.

The law of life is not a separate agent working independently of mankind and separate from individual life.

Man himself is a phase of the great law in operation. When he once fully awakens to the universal co-operation of the attributes and thoughts through which the great dynamo operates or preceeds, he an Ego one of the expressions of infinity, will be enabled to free himself from the seeming environments of matter, and thus realizing his power, will assert his dominion over all he has been an agent in creating. And he has indeed assisted in creating manifesting all that is. Being a thought, an outbreathing of universal spirit, he is co-eternal with it.

In material concept, we do not begin to realize the extent of our wisdom. When we awaken to Egos, or spirit, consciousness knowledge that we are Egos that have bodies or temples, and not bodies that have Egos we see the object or reason of all symbols or manifestation, and begin to realize our own power over all created things.

And in this Aquarian age, great changes in nature's laws will be speedily brought to pass, and great changes in the affairs of humanity will result. The laws of vibration will be mastered, and through their operation material manifestations will be shaped and moulded to man's will. It is only a matter of time when all the necessities of life will be produced directly from the elements of the air.

It is well known by chemists that all manner of fruits, grains and vegetables are produced directly from the elements in the air, and not from the soil. The earth, of course, serves as a negative pole and furnishes the mineral salts of lime, magnesium, iron, potassium, sodium and silica, which act as carriers of water, oil, sugar, albumen, etc., and are formed by a precipitation or condensation of principles in the air, and not from the soil. This is a fact abundantly proved. Mr. Berthelot, a scientist of France, Tesla, the Austrian wizard, and our own Edison have long held that food can be produced artificially by a synthetic process from its elements. Some six or seven extracts, as well as coloring material, are now being manufactured in this manner. Madder is made almost exclusively by this process now.

Mr. Berthelot, at one time the French minister of foreign affairs, possesses fame apart altogether from his political efforts. In his special domain of chemical knowledge he ranks among the first of his contemporaries. Chemical synthesis the science of artificially putting organized bodies together may be said to owe its existence to him. The practical results expected to flow from his experiments and discoveries are enormous. Thus, sugar has recently been made in the laboratory from glycerine, which Professor Berthelot first made direct from synthetic alcohol. Commerce has now taken up the question; and an invention has recently been patented by which sugar is to be made upon a commercial scale, from two gases, at something like 1 cent per pound. M. Berthelot declares he has not the slightest doubt that sugar will eventually be manufactured on a large scale synthetically, and that the culture of sugar cane and beet root will be abandoned, because they have ceased to pay.

The chemical advantages promised by M. Berthelot to future generations are marvelous. He cites the case of alzarin, a compound whose synthetic manufacture by chemists has destroyed a great agricultural industry. It is the essential commercial principle of the madder root, which was once used in dyeing, wherever any dyeing was going on. The chemists have now succeeded in making pure indigo direct from its elements, and it will soon be a commercial product. Then the indigo field, like the madder fields, will be abandoned, industrial laboratories having usurped their place.

But these scientific wonders do not stop here. Tobacco, tea and coffee are to be made artificially; not only this, but there is substantial promise that such tobacco, such teas and such coffees as the world has never seen will be the outcome. Theobromine, the essential principle of cocoa, has been produced in the laboratory, thus synthetic chemistry is getting ready to furnish the three great non-alcoholic beverages now in general use.

Biochemists long ago advanced the theory that animal tissue is formed from the air inhaled, and not from food.

The food, of course, serves its purpose; it acts as the negative pole, as does the earth to plant and vegetable life, and also furnishes the inorganic salts, the workers that carry on the chemistry of life, setting free magnetism, heat and electric forces by disintegration and fermentation of the organic portions of the food.

But air, in passing through the various avenues and complex structure of the human organism, changes, condenses, solidifies, until it is finally deposited as flesh and bone. From this established scientific truth, it appears that, by constructing a set of tubes, pumps, etc., resembling the circulatory system, as well as the lung cells of the human mechanism, which is a chemical laboratory, where the chemistry of spirit is ever at work, changing the one essence of spirit substance to blood, flesh and bone, air may be changed into an albuminous pabulum, which may be again changed into the special kind of food required by adding the proper flavor, which may also be produced direct from the air.

There does not seem to be any reason why this substance, the basis of all food or vegetable growth, cannot, by drying and proper process, be made into material for clothing. Wool, cotton, flax, silks, etc., are all produced from the universal elements through the slow, laborious and costly process of animal or vegetable growth. Why not produce them directly?

Those who believe in a time of peace on earth, a millennial reign, certainly do not think that our present mode of producing food will continue during that age. Slaughter of animals, and fruit, grain or vegetable raising, leave small time for men and women to enjoy a condition foretold by all the seers and prophets. But under the new way of producing food and clothing, the millennium is possible. And thus will the problem of subsistence be solved. No more monopoly of nature's bounties. An exchange of service will be the coin of the world instead of certain metals difficult to obtain.

A realization of this vision, or theory, that will for awhile be called visionary by most people, will mean Eden restored.

Many people have wondered why, during the last few years, fruit pests have multiplied so alarmingly, and why cows are almost universally diseased and so much attention given to meat, milk, and butter products by Boards of Health, etc. There is surely a reason for all this. The One Life, Supreme Intelligence, or Divine Wisdom, that holds the worlds of space in their appointed orbits, surely knows all about the affairs of earth. When a new dispensation is about to be

24

ushered in, old things begin to pass away.

All labor of preparing food and clothing, as now carried on, will cease, and the people, in governmental or collective capacity, will manufacture and distribute all manner of food and clothing free. Machinery for the production of everything necessary for man's material wants will be simple and easily manipulated. One-twentieth of the able-bodied population, working one or two hours a day, and shifting every week, or day, for that matter, with others, will produce an abundant supply. Neither droughts nor floods nor winter's snow can affect the supply. It can be made in Klondyke or the Tropics. Garments may be worn for a few days and then burned, and laundry work cease. Cooking will be reduced to a minimum, as the food will only need flavoring. No preparing vegetables, fruits, or cracking nuts; no making butter, or preserving meats. Men will not have to devote their lives to the endless grind of food production, nor woman to cooking, dish-washing, sewing, and laundry-work. Garments of beautiful design and finest texture will be made by machines invented for the purpose, ready for wear.

A dream, you say? I cannot admit that, in the face of the indisputable evidence it has already been able to produce, but what, if it were, at present, but the dream it may appear to be to the one who hears of its methods of operation for the first time, it is certain of future fulfillment. Do dreams ever come true? Yea, verily! All concrete facts are materialized dreams.

An Egyptian King dreamed, and the Pyramids of Cheops mass and miracle his vision. The Pyramids are encyclopedic of physical science and astral lore. The science of numbers, weights, measures, geometry, astronomy, astrology, and all the deeper mysteries of the human body and soul are symboled in these incomparable monuments.

A dream of an ancient alchemist solidified in stone, and the awful sphinx sat down in Egypt's sand to gaze into eternity.

Columbus dreamed, and a white-sailed ship turned its prow west and west. On uncharted seas, with an eternity of water ahead, he remembered his dream, and answered "Sail on !" to the discouraged mate, until he landed on the unknown shores of a most wonderful new world.

Michael Angelo dreamed a thousand dreams and sleeping marble awoke and smiled. Hudson and Fulton dreamed, and steamboats "run over and under the seas."

The Pilgrim Fathers dreamed and America, the "marvel of nations," banners the skies with the stars and stripes. Marcus Whitman and Lewis and Clarke dreamed long and hard and the bones of oxen and men and women and babies made a bridge over the desert sands and the mountain gorges to the shores of the Sundown Sea, and now the Pullman cars come safely over. Morse and Marconi and Edison dreamed strange wild dreams and concentrated intelligence springs from carbon-crucible and says to earth's boundaries, "Lo; here am I."

> Vibration of etheric substance
>   Causing light through regions of space,
> A girdle of something enfolding
>   And binding together the race—
> And words without wires transmitted,
>   Aerial-winged, spirit-sandalled and shod:
> Some call it electricity,
>   And others call it God !

A mechanic dreamed, and sprang upon his automobile, and drove it till the axles blazed and the spaces shriveled behind him. Men of high strung airy brains dreamed wondrous dreams, and now the eagle's highway and the open road of men lie parallel.

A musician dreamed a sweet, harmonious dream, and forth from a throat of brass directed by a million tiny fingers of steel, came the entrancing notes that have run riot through the singer's brain.

So let us dream on, men and women, of the day of rest that is already dawning in the heavens. No wonder that Paul said, "Now, brethren, are we the Sons of God, but it doth not yet appear what we shall be," as such. The morning light of that glad day now purples the mountains of faith and hope with its rays of glory.

And when Man is once fully alive to his own heritage, realizing the wonders and possibilities of his own body, and the power of his spirit to control it, and to provide for its needs, he will assert the divine right within him to be a spirit in command of its own temple, and the environment of that temple, and will rejoice in the revealed truth of his own divinity that alone can make him free.

TRANSMUTATION,
OR TURNING WATER INTO WINE

The Lord of transmutation has ascended the throne of Aquarius to rule the world for 2000 years.

Aquarius the fifth Son (Sun) of Jacob, circle, or to follow after, is Dan, Hebrew for Judge. Thus the day or time of judgment or understanding will have for its executor the revolutionary Planet Uranus, or as it is in Greek "Oranous." Uranus virtually means Son of Heaven.

This god is surely a suitable ruler for the Zodiacal Sign Aquarius the Man. "And then shall appear the Sign of the Son (Sun) of man in the Heavens."

The Solar System now being in Aquarius we may expect, and as a matter of fact, are experiencing the prophecies of great Astrologians as recorded in Matt. 24th, also Luke 21st.

In the Judgment Day, or time of knowledge, we are due to realize the process by which base metals are transmuted into gold.

The word gold comes from Or, a product of the Sun's rays, or the breath of life.

Life or Spirit breathed into man precipitates brain cells and gray matter which creates or builds the fluids and structure of physical man.

Or, is the seed or the Word—Lord, etc.

"In the beginning was the word God." ... the word was God."

Even our great Theologians have admitted that God means Power.

Thus the emanations from Sun, basic material, are changed to gold and the process, eternally proceeding, is being recognized by man at the present day, due to the fact that the Planet of gold, Oranous, is now ruling Earth and thereby bringing good judgment upon the people, and the thrones and scepters of rulers lie scattered and crushed along the highway of Nations.

Both in Greek and Hebrew any fluid, air or ether was called water until organized; then it was wine. The rain that falls on the ground and is taken up into the organism of tree, vegetable or fruit is changed into wine, i. e., sap or juice. The parable of turning water into wine at the marriage at Cana in Galilee is a literal statement of a process taking place every heart beat in the human organism.

Galilee means a circle of water or fluid—the circulatory system. Cana means a dividing place, the lungs or reeds, the tissue and cells of the lungs.

Biochemists have shown that food does not form the organic part of blood, but simply furnishes the mineral base by setting free the inorganic or cell-salts contained in all food-stuff. The organic part, oil, fibrin, albumen, etc., contained in food is burned or digested in the stomach and intestinal tract to furnish motive power to operate the human machine and draw air into lungs, or Cana, thence into the arteries, i. e., air carriers. Therefore, it is clearly shown that air (spirit) unites with the minerals and forms blood, proving that the oil, albumen, etc., found in blood, is created every breath at the "marriage in Cana of Galilee."

Air was called water or the pure sea, viz. : Virgin Mary. So we see how water is changed into wine—blood—every moment.

In the new age, we will need perfect bodies to correspond with higher vibration, or motion of the new blood, for "old bottles (bodies) , cannot contain the new wine."

Another allegorical statement typifying the same truth reads, "And I saw a new Heaven and a New Earth," i. e., new mind and new body.

Biochemistry may well say with Walt Whitman, "To the sick lying on their backs I bring help, and to the strong upright man I bring much needed help." To be grouchy, cross, irritable, despondent or easily discouraged, is prima facie evidence that the fluids of the stomach, liver and brain are not vibrating at normal rate, the rate that results in equilibrium or health. Health cannot be qualified, i. e., poor health or good health. There must be either health or dis-health; ease or disease. We do not say poor ease or good ease.

We say ease or dis-ease, viz., not at ease.

A sufficient amount of the cell-salts of the body properly combined and taken as food—not simply to cure some ache, pain or exudation—forms blood that materializes in healthy fluids, flesh and bone tissue.

We should take the tissue cell-salts as one uses health foods, not simply to change, not health to health, but to keep the rate of blood vibration in the tone of health all the time.

Biochemistry is the sign board pointing to the open country, to hills and green fields of health and the truth that shall set the seeking Ego free from poverty and disease. Conservation and transmutation obtains in all the commercial world. The force of falling water is transmuted into the product of the factories. Steam, the vibration of copper and carbon discs that turn night into day, the "chariots that run like lightning and jostle each other in the streets" are the effects of the transmutation of base or basic material.

On some fair tomorrow when the subtle vibrations of the Aquarian Age, directed by Oranous shall have awakened and called to action the millions of dormant cells of the wondrous brain, man will, by the power of the lost word, conserve and transmute the material substance of his body, the soul, I O H N or JOHN, and with the "product," the precious ointment oil triumph over the cross at Golgotha and ascend to the pineal gland that transmits the christed Son to the Optic Thalmus, the all-seeing Eye of the chamber and thus furnish "light to all that are in the house."

In these latter days our business world has been dominated by a great oil trust, and petroleum, mineral oil, petra, stone, rock or mineral and oleum-oil was exploited by Rockefeller, a mineral fellow, and then by the laws of transmutation changed into gasoline.

The transmutation of gasoline by the miracle of the "conservation of energy" causes the "Ascension" of the air ship, and the pathway of the Eagle and the open road of man lie parallel across the vaulted sky.

And when the Ego shall have triumphed over the carnal mind and transmuted the crude soul fluids into the gold of the "New Wine" it will ascend to the Father, the upper brain.

"And the temple needs no light of the Sun by day nor moon by night, for the light of the Lord doth lighten it."

Thus will the "Blood of Christ cleanse from all sin."

Our Lord Oranous, Son of Heaven, ruling the Sign of the Son of man, may then exclaim, "I have fought the good fight, I have finished my course."

PSYCHOMETRY

The word psychometry was coined by the noted scientist, Joseph Rhodes Buchanan . It is derived from psycho , or Psuche, the Greek for soul, and mitron , meter , to measure. Therefore, the word psychometry means literally soul measurement. Soul is from the Hebrew Nephesh , meaning breath, and the Greek word Psuche,—breath.

"God breathed into man the breath of life and he became a living soul."

Thus every atom of the body is Soul Stuff and the complete body is the soul that can b e saved or lost. While the entire body is soul, the scriptures refer, in most instances to the nerve fluids, gray matter of the brain and marrow of the spinal cord (River of Jordan) as soul.

The word breath is translated soul more than 500 times in the bible . Paul writes of body , soul and spirit.

The contention that psychometry is a science, and therefore worthy of recognition, is sustained by two indisputable facts. First, chemists all agree that there is but one substance in the universe , which in different degrees of fineness, attenuation or rates of motion, causes all appearances, all forms, all that we see, hear, feel, smell, or in any way sense, thus corroborating Herbert Spencer's statement that "all things proceed from one universal energy."

Second fact : Every person who is at all sensitive to impressions is more or less affected by the influence, the aura, of clothing, of works of art, or any product of man's hands, as well as natural products, but more especially are they affected by reading the written or spoken words of individuals.

No theory seems better established as a fact, than the theory that the particular vibration, or degree of intensity of thought, or the particular quality of a writer or speaker, is transmitted to the reader or listener.

We are not yet able to tell by what subtle, wireless telegraphy, chemical affinity, or alchemical transmutation, this marvelous operation is performed; but we must recognize the fact.

Chemistry is now merging into alchemy, from which it originally sprung. Modern chemistry is but the material side or effect of alchemy. All real scientists and especially the advanced chemists agree that the universal substance in its higher rate of motion, constitutes the higher intelligence, spirit or energy.

Other or lower rates of activity manifest in the gases, water, vegetable, wood, stone, etc., etc.

Thus, ice is crystallized or frozen water while water is itself a product of rates of motion called oxygen and hydrogen—two of hydrogen to one of oxygen.

But water disappears when the two gases are set free or separated.

The new chemistry has discovered the truth that all gases, all so-called elements, can be split, chemically, and resolved into the unknown and unamenable Absolute.

The spiritual scientist does not recognize law as a separate agent from himself, but being "led by the spirit" he fully realizes that he is himself a phase of the law in operation.

By thus recognizing the universal co-operation of the attributes or thoughts through which the great Dynamis operates or proceeds, you, a spiritual entity, one of the thoughts or words of God, are enabled to free yourself from the seeming environments of matter and thus realize your dominion over all you have been an agent in creating.

And you have assisted in creating—manifesting—all that is.

Being a thought, an outbreathing of universal spirit, you are co-eternal with it. The substance everywhere, omnipresent, was of course never created.

These thought-vibrations are materialized, analyzed, understood and described as a painter explains the effects, lights and shades of his pictures, or a mechanic the results of his handiwork.

In material concept we do not realize the extent of our wisdom. When we awaken to spirit, consciousness—knowledge that we are Egos that have bodies or temples and not bodies that have Egos—we see the object or reason of all symbols or manifestations, or formed things, and we spell the words again and this is called psychometry.

With a full understanding of the Oneness of life, and that all life is but a phase of Eternal Life, comes the power to psychometrize. If we can cognize the great truth that the products of nature are likewise the results of our own intelligence, we begin to see why it is possible to read the history of a certain article by coming in touch with its vibrations.

Let us make the proper distinction between reason and intuition. Intuition is knowing. Reason is only a supposition, that a certain thing or theory is true. If it be demonstrated that the theory is false, the structure or argument built upon the sand-formation of reason, falls. Intuition does not depend upon reason or so-called logical deductions.

To psychometrize we should wait for "the still small voice" of intuition, and not attempt to find truth by the material roads of reason and logic.

Relax all bodily functions and thus quiet material operation and you may read so-called inert matter, as you would read printed pages. Psychometry is miracle made natural, or occultism engrafted into everyday life.

"Nothing is hidden that shall not be revealed," and humanity stands at the door of the New Day when "none shall say unto his neighbor, "Know the Lord," for all shall know Truth and Truth shall set them free."

IT:
THE ETERNITY OF PERFECTION

A child brought to its mother a piece of ice, and asked: "What is this?"

The mother answered, "it is ice."

Again the child asked, "What is there in ice?" The child desired to find the water in the ice,

and it procured a hammer, and pounded the piece of ice into little bits and the warm air soon changed all the ice to water. The child was grievously disappointed, for the ice that the child supposed contained water had disappeared.

And the child said, "Where is the ice that contained this water?"

And so it came to pass that the mother was compelled, by the child's persistent questions, to say, "ice is all water; there is no such thing as ice ; that which we call ice is crystalized or frozen water."

The child understood.

A student brought to his teacher some water and asked, "What is water? What does it contain?"

The teacher answered, "Water contains oxygen and hydrogen," and then explained how the two gases might be separated and set free by heat.

The student boiled the water until all of the molecules of oxygen and hydrogen had been set free, but he was surprised to find that all of the water had disappeared.

Then the student asked of the teacher, "Where is the water that held the gases that have escaped?"

Then was the teacher compelled by the student's persistent questions to answer, "Water itself is the product of oxygen and hydrogen. Water does not contain anything other than these gases. In reality, there is no such substance or fluid as water; that which we name water is a rate of motion set in operation by the union of two parts of hydrogen with one part of oxygen, and of course the phenomenon disappears when the union of the gases is broken."

The student understood.

A devout scientist presented himself before God and said, "Lord, what are these gases men call oxygen and hydrogen?"

The good Lord answered and said, "They are molecules in the blood and body of the universe."

Then spake the scientist, "Lord, wilt thou tell me of the kind of molecules that compose Thy blood and body?"

The Lord replied, "These same molecules, gases or principles, compose my blood and body; for I and the universe are one and the same."

Once again the scientist said, "My Lord, may I ask, then, what is spirit and what is matter?"

And thus answered the Lord :

"As ice and water are one, and the gases and water are one, so is spirit and matter one. The different phases and manifestations cognized by man in the molecules of My body— that is, the universe,— are caused by the Word; thus, they are My thoughts clothed with form."

Now the scientist felt bold, being redeemed from fear, and asked "is my blood, then, identical with Thy blood in composition and Divine Essence?"

And the Lord said, "Yea, thou art one with the Father." The scientist now understood and said, "Now mine eyes are opened, and I perceive that when I eat, I partake of Thy body; when I drink, I drink of Thy blood; and when I breathe, I breathe Thy spirit."

So-called matter is Pure Intelligence and nothing else—because there is not anything else.

Pure intelligence cannot progress or becomes better. There is nothing but Intelligence. Omnipresence, Omnipotence, Omniscience must mean Intelligence; therefore these terms are all included in the word.

Let us adopt a short word that will express all that the above written words are intended to express, namely, the word IT. "I" stands for all—the eternal I. "T" stands for operation, manifestation, vibration, action or motion. The "I" in motion is "T," or Crossification, viz., the T-cross. We say, "IT" rains!" "IT is cold!" "IT is all right!" What do we mean by "It?" Who knows? Some say, "The weather !" Others, "Natural phenomena!" Very well, then,—what do we mean by "the weather," or "natural phenomena" ? Why, just It, of course !

IT does not progress; it does not need to. IT forever manifests, operates, differentiates and presents different aspects or viewpoints of ITSELF. But these different phases are neither good, better nor best, neither bad nor worse—simply different shades and colorings of the One and Only Intelligence.

Every so-called thing, whether it be animal, vegetable, or mineral, molecule or atom, ion or electron, is the result of the One Intelligence expressing itself in different rates of motion. Then what is Spirit?

Spirit means breath or life. Spirit, that which is breathed into man, must be intelligence, or man would not be intelligent. Non-intelligent substance, which is, of course, unthinkable, would not breathe into anything, nor make it intelligent if it did. Therefore we see that Spirit, Intelligence and Matter are one and the same Esse in different rates of motion.

So-called molecules, atoms, electrons, know what to do.

They know where and how to cohere, unite, and operate to form a leaf or a flower. They know how to separate and disintegrate that same leaf or flower. These particles of omnipresent life build planets, suns, and systems; they hurl the comet on its way across measureless deserts of star-dust, and emboss its burning path.

From the materialistic and individual concept of life and its operations, it is pitiable and pathetic to view the wrecks along the shores of science. It is only when we view these apparently sad failures from the firm foothold of the unity of being and the operation of wisdom that we clearly see in these frictions and warring elements and temporary defeats and victories the chemical operation of Eternal Spirit—operating with its own substance its very self. It is only

through the fires of transmutation that we are enabled to see that all life is one Eternal Life and therefore cannot be taken, injured, or destroyed.

The fitful, varying, changing beliefs of men in the transition stage from the sleep and dreams of materialism to the realization of the Oneness of Spirit show forth in a babel of words and theories, a few of which I shall briefly consider, beginning with the yet popular belief in Evolution :

The evolutionary concept has its starting point in the idea (a) that matter—so-called—is a something separate from mind, intelligence, or Spirit; (b) that this matter had a beginning; (c) that it contains within itself the desire to progress or improve; and finally, that the race is progressing, becoming wiser, better, etc.

Against this assumption, I submit the proposition that the Universe,—one verse,—always existed without beginning or ending, and is and always has been absolutely perfect in all its varied manifestations and operations.

A machine is no stronger than its weakest part. If the self-existing universe is weak or imperfect in any part, it must, of necessity, always have been so. Having all the knowledge there—is being all,—it is unthinkable that there is any imperfection anywhere. Everything we see, feel, or taste, or in any manner sense, is perfect substance, condensed or manifested from perfect elements, but all differ in their notes, vibrations, or modes or rates of motion. A serpent is as perfect, therefore as good, as a man. Without feet, it outruns a man; without hands, it outclimbs the ape, and has been a symbol of wisdom through all the ages. Man is an evil thing to the serpent's consciousness. Neither are evil—nor good. They are different expressions or variations of the "Play of the Infinite Will."

The brain of the jelly-fish is composed of the same elements, of the same substance as the brain of a man, merely of a different combination. Can man tell what the jelly-fish is thinking, or why it moves and manifests its energy thus or so? How, then, is man wiser than the jelly-fish because his thoughts are of a different nature, and operate to different ends?

Wisdom—all there is—simply operates, manifests, expresses forms, or creates with, or of, self-existing substance. As wisdom is without beginning or end, so are all its operations or manifestations without beginning or end. If the race is constantly evolving to higher standards and loftier conceptions, why send young men and women to Rome and Florence to study the "Old Masters?" If man has evolved up from the "lower forms of life," why has he spent so much time, money, and brain energy in trying to understand these lower forms, and to do what they do? Why does he not remember and retain the power of his earlier states of manifestation?

The eagle must wonder, as it watches man's efforts and failures to perfect his flying machine, how long it will be before he evolves up to the science of the birds, i. e., the science of flying. Modern man is now taking his first lessons in condensing or materializing air, while through unnumbered ages the spider has performed the miracle without the necessity of first attending a school of chemistry. The modus operandi by which the spider forms his web from air is the despair of science. The wisdom of the ant or beaver strikes dumb all the believers in the Darwinian dream. The perfect co-operative commonwealth of the bees is still the unattained ideal of man.

Beneath the soil upon which falls the shadow of the throne of Menelik, the Abyssinian King, are layers and strata of buried civilizations, and astronomers in China mapped the Heavens, named the stars, calculated eclipses and the return of comets ages before Moses led the Hebrews out of bondage, or the walls of Baalbeck cast a shade for the Arab and his camel.

The evidences and witnesses of the wisdom of men on earth hundreds of thousands of years ago confront the scientific investigator at every turn. Here the Rossetta Stone, and there the Inscribed Cylinder of Arioch or Statue of Gudea, King of Chaldea. Prophecies, inscribed on Cunieform tablets of Clay, foretelling the building of the Pyramids, are brought to light by the excavator; and the history of the Chinese Empire, running back in links of an unbroken chain for one hundred and fifty thousand years, forever refute the theory of the "Descent of Man !" Side by side with the ancient Asiatics who knew all that we today know, dwelt the Crystal, the Cell, the Jelly-Fish, the Saurian, the Ape, and the Cave-Man. Side by side with the masons who could build arches of stone in ancient Yucatan that mock at the ravages of Time, lived and wrought the ant, operating in its co-operative commonwealth of which man can still only dream. Side by side with the cave men and cannibals dwells the spider, whose operation in aerial elements is the despair of chemical investigators. And when Solomon's golden-spired temple illuminated the Holy City, or the tower of Babel grew toward the clouds, or the Mound Builders recorded their history in rock and soil, the eagle and the dove calmly floated in the air and wondered when men would evolve to their plane of science. They are wondering still.

Exponents of the evolutionary theory never tire in quoting Professor Huxley. One who has no tread the writings of this eminent scientist would be led to believe by the statements of his followers that he had positive views on the great question of force and matter. Following is an extract from a letter written by Professor Huxley to Charles Kingsley, under date of May 22nd, 1863, taken from the published letters of Huxley by his son, Leonard :

"I don't know whether Matter is anything distinct from Force. I don't know that atoms are anything but pure myths —'Cogito ergo sum' is to my mind a ridiculous piece of bad logic, all I can say at any time being 'Cogito.' The Latin form I hold to be preferable to the English 'I think,' because the latter asserts the existence of an Ego about which the bundle of phenomena at present addressing you knows nothing. I believe in Hamilton, Mansell, and Herbert Spenser, so long as they are destructive, and laugh at their beards as soon as they try to spin their own cobwebs.

"Is this basis of ignorance broad enough for you? If you, theologian, can find as firm footing as I, man of science, do on this foundation of minus naught—there will be naught to fear for our ever diverging. For you see, I am quite as ready to admit your doctrine that souls secrete bodies as I am the opposite one that bodies secrete souls—simply because I deny the possibility of obtaining any evidence as to the truth or falsehood of either hypothesis. My fundamental axiom of speculative philosophy is that materialism

and spiritualism are opposite poles of the same absurdity— the absurdity of imagining that we know anything about either spirit or matter."

Huxley admitted that he did not know.

As the appetite craves new chemical combinations of food from day to day, so does mind crave new concepts of infinite life. The word "Infinite" defines an endless differentiation of concept.

If the Spiritual Consciousness, the "mighty Angel" that the clairvoyant seer, John the Revelator, saw descending out of the Heavens, shall carry away the pillars of material evolution, a Temple of Truth divinely fair will spring, Phoenix-like, to take its place. Eyes shall then be opened, and ears unstopped. Man will then realize that the so-called lower forms of life are just as complex, wonderful, and difficult to form as the organism of man that protoplasm is as wonderful in any other form as in the gray matter of the human brain, which is only another form of its expression,—that the molecular composition of a jelly-fish puzzles the greatest chemist, and the wisdom of a beaver is enough to strike dumb all the believers in the Darwinian fairy tale.

And has the dream of good and evil any better foundation than has this one of material evolution? We are here to solve the problems of life, not to evade them; and to name the mighty operations of Eternal Wisdom good and evil is simply evading instead of solving.

The universal Principle, Spirit, or God, is impartial. Saint and Sinner are one in the Eternal Mind. God, or Infinite Life is not in the least injured by so-called good or evil. The Spiritual Ego is the interested party and must work out its own Salvation. There is no point in the universe better, higher, or nearer God, or the centre, than any other point. All places are necessary, and no one is favored over any other. As Huxley well said, "Good and evil are opposite poles of the same absurdity." Good must have evil for its opposite, if it exists at all. He who would realize Being must get rid of the concept of good, as well as the concept of evil. Good and evil are qualifications, and Being does not admit of qualification or grades. It simply is. The ideal we call good eternally exists, but its name is wisdom's operations. Nothing is low or high, good or bad, except to individual concept that allows comparison. "Comparisons are odious."

Physical Science, so-called, declares in its text-books that light travels from the sun to the earth in eight minutes, a distance of about ninety-five million miles. To question this statement a few years ago meant ostracism from the circle of the elect who knew things. But today the iconoclast stands at the gate of the temples of learning and batters at the walls with the hammer of Thor. Fear and trembling seize upon the votaries of material gods as they see evolution, progression, the theories of electricity, light, and heat, good and evil, all cast into the crucible of truth for transmutation in the Divine Alchemy of Being, all dissolving as pieces of ice of different sizes and shapes change to water.

The present day chemist, as he begins to tread the soil where stood the ancient alchemist, tells us that light and heat are simply rates of motion of a substance that does not travel from star to star or from sun to planet, but vibrates in its place at rates directed by the Eternal Word. This substance, aerial or etheric, does not travel—it is everywhere present—the body of omnipresent being.

Men now dare assert that there is no evidence that the sun is hot, but that there is evidence that the sun is the dynamo of the Solar System and so vibrates the etheric substance that light, heat, cold and gravitation are produced, not as entities separate from the universal elements, but as results or effects produced by different rates of motion of the molecules of the wire—molecular motion—or of the air or etheric substance, as in wireless telegraphy.

Another ancient belief, now obsolete, is the progression of man in a better state of existence after death or cessation of bodily functions. This idea had its origin in the fallacy that there were grades of goodness in the Divine Mind, and that somehow we are not treated right during earth life, and that, in consequence, we must be rewarded by an easy berth "over there." But we now see quite clearly that the great cause of life and all its operations would be unjust to withhold from its sons and daughters for one moment anything that belonged to them. If the Cause ever does wrong, we see no reason why it should repent and do right. If the Cause ever failed in the least particular to give just dues, it may do so again at any time. The "better state of existence" mentioned above can only come through wisdom obtained here and now; thus will man "work out his own salvation."

The time was, and not so very long ago, when the recognized scientist believed that there were about seventy-four elements, indivisible, separate, and distinct; but the alchemical iconoclast with his hammer of truth has pulverized the fallacy and remorselessly hammered and pounded the seventy-four faces into one countenance.

For a long time, hydrogen gas, the negative pole of water, was supposed to be indivisible beyond all question; but the present day chemist knows it is only an expression of yet more subtle molecules back of which, "Standeth God within the shadow keeping watch above His own."

A post mortem examination of some of the wreck's along the shores of the troubled sea of science discloses a belief that the Ego is an individual, who through knowledge of its divine origin may draw unto itself all things it may desire ! But as fast as the Sleepers awaken they see that each Ego is only "part of one stupendous whole" that does not draw unto itself anything. That there is no law of attraction for the eternal substance is everywhere present and each one uses exactly that portion prepared for him from everlasting unto everlasting.

When the continuity of life was first demonstrated beyond question those who caught the first dispatches from disincarnate spirits sprang forth from their beds of material sleep and with half-opened eyes only saw the great truth through "a glass darkly." Then came a babel of words. They jabbered a jargon that needed translation to be understood. The ideas of progression in earth life that obtained among men was transplanted to the spirit realm and we were told by the votaries of spiritual philosophy that men and women had great opportunities for progression after leaving the flesh.

As the idea of a commencement of the universe was a common belief among those asleep in material consciousness, being the corner stone of evolution, so the idea obtained that the individual had a commencement in the maternal human laboratory. As these half-awakened individuals could not comprehend that an action contrary to their concept of good could possibly be caused by Infinite Intelligence they concluded that the so-called bad actions of men and women were prompted by evil earth-bound spirits. These people — many of them—also thought that the main object of the existence of Spirits in the Spirit realm was to gather information about mines, and stocks, and bonds, and lotteries, and races and thus assist poor mortals to get-rich-quick. It was supposed that these spirits were posted in regard to deeds and wills and knew when wealthy relatives would shuffle off the mortal coil or when undesirable wives or husbands would "pass out."

But at last the sun of Truth pierced the darkness and the jargon of selfishness changed to the "New Song." We now clearly see that each spirit is a part or attribute of the One Eternal Spirit therefore has existed always and that the process of generation deals with flesh clothing, or mask for the spirit in which it performs a necessary part in the creative process. The word "person" is derived from a Greek word, Persona, meaning mask.

We see that the phenomena we have called obsession by evil spirits is God's surgery or dynamic operation in his own temple quite as impossible for us to understand in our present environment as it is for the child to understand the wisdom and necessity in the operation of the adept surgeon. And, finally, we now see and realize fully that Eternal Wisdom without beginning or end of days does not progress before entering a temple of flesh, while it occupies it, or after it leaves it. All creative or formative processes may properly be termed operations of wisdom or Eternal Life.

In the unwalled temple of the Now, beneath its roofless dome there is no progression, but a constantly moving panorama forever presenting to consciousness new phases of the absolute.

The men and women who do things take hold of opportunities and material that they find all about them now, and operate with them, astonishing results following the efforts of all who recognize that eternal force has use for them NOW to carry out the divine plan. We are all operators or workmen in the divine workshop, and the Divine Intelligence, the eternal IT, made no mistake in placing any of us here, but does insist that we recognize that NOW is the time and Here is the place to do our best. As the Great Cause does not need to first practice on lower forms in order at some future time to attain perfection, we must recognize and practice being in the present, instead of becoming in the future, for the Eternal Now is all the time there is.

"But," you say, "your science has taken away my God, and I know not where you have lain Him." On the contrary, I have brought you to the one true God, "which was, and is, and evermore shall be."

The fifth verse of the last chapter of the book of Job reads as follows :

"I have heard of thee by the hearing of the ear; but now mine eye seeth thee."

The wonderful writings and scientific statements found in that Book of all books, the Christian Bible, were recorded at dates covering thousands of years by men and women who never heard of each other. Some of these teachers lived away back in the age when the solar system was swinging through the zodiacal sign,Taurus; when Phallic worship prevailed; when the number six was understood as sex, and the creative or formative principle operating through the sex functions was worshipped as the very Holy of Holies. Other teachers who contributed to the knowledge of life and its operations contained in the Bible, lived in the age of Aries, a fire sign, when fire and sun were worshipped as the essence of God; and as heat, the cause of the phenomenon called fire, cannot be seen, it was a reasonable thing to say that "no one can see God and live." So then, it depends upon the point of view one has of God, or the spirit of things, whether he says, "No one can see God and live," or says, "Now mine eye seeth thee!"

I think the writer of the book named Job must have lived more than eight thousand years ago, even before the Taurian age—symbolized by the Winged Bull of Nineveh—which was in the Gemini age, the age of perception and expression, being an air age. Let it be understood that an age in this connection means twenty-two hundred years, the period for the solar system to pass across one of the signs of the zodiac. In an air age, Egos awaken to their divine heritage, and realize their Godhood. The writer of Job, then, living in the Gemini or air age, could see God and live. Our solar system has entered the sign Aquarius, another air sign, and the spiritualized elements so act upon our brain-cells that we are able to understand the teachers of a past air age, and also see God and live.

Carlyle, the prince of literary critics, said "The book of Job is the most wonderful and beautiful literary production ever given to the world." Certainly the scientific truths of astrology and alchemy, and of the Spirit's operation in flesh, as set forth in that book, are without a parallel. The letters J, O, B, have an occult, scientific meaning, I and J are the same IOB meaning the same as JOB. I means the Eternal I. All the Hebrew letters were formed from I. O means the universe, without beginning or end, and B means Beth, a body, house, church, or temple. Therefore, GOD, or all, maybe discovered as seen in JOB or IOB. The word, Job, has no reference to a person. The name, or letters of the word, symbolize principle, the same as wisdom, knowledge, intelligence, or Christ, or Buddha. We symbolize the principles of our government in personalities, and picture them in the form of a man or woman, namely, Uncle Sam, or Columbia. But we do more than that: we put words in their mouth, and make them utter speech. And shall we ignore these facts when dealing with the record of past ages? One record plainly states that Jesus spake only in parables.

But let us consider more closely the discovery of God. The numerical value of G.O.D., according to ancient Kabala, is nine the all of mathematics no person is alluded to. If the statement, "I and the Father are one," is true, the "I" must be the Father manifested or expressed. As it is not possible to conceive of the Father except through expression, we must conclude that manifestation in some form of so called matter is eternal—the great necessity—and has therefore always been.

It is quite reasonable to think that some oxygen and hydrogen has eternally existed in gaseous form, some in the combination that causes water and some in the concrete or concentrated form known as ice. Then upon the postulate that Spirit and matter—that is, bodily or material expression—are one, it follows logically that matter, including the physical body or temple of man, is as necessary to the Father-Mother principle while held in a given rate of activity or expression as this life essence is necessary to matter, or the physical structure of man. I see oxygen and hydrogen when I look at the manifestation we call ice. When I see water, I know just how oxygen and hydrogen appear when united. So when I look at any form of so-called matter, I know exactly how God appears at that particular time and place. I do not see the effect or works of God, but I see God, and just as much of God, face to face, as I am capable of seeing or recognizing at a certain time.

Step by step, the scientific investigator is being led to the threshold of the awful, absolute Truth, that all matter, or substance, or energy or force,—call it what you may—is not only intelligent, but is Pure Intelligence itself. Atoms, molecules, electrons are but expressions of rates of motion of pure Mind, Thought, or Intelligence that man has personified and called God. Ice is not permeated with water, or controlled by water. Ice is water. Matter is not controlled by mind; mind and matter are one. A high vibration of mind does control, to a certain extent, a lower vibration of mind, as water may carry a lump of ice here or there, water being a more positive rate of activity of the same thing. The particles, so-called, of matter know what to do. The atoms that compose a leaf know when to cohere and materialize a leaf, and they know how and when to disintegrate and dematerialize it : "Thou shalt have no others gods."

I hold in my hand that particular form of the one thing called a rose. Material thought says it is made by God, or that God is in the rose or back of it, or that God caused or created it; but when Spirit, the I Am, asks where is the God that created the rose, where has he betaken Himself, material belief is silent. But hold a moment! I have here a bud, a half-formed rose. If God makes a rose, He must continue the work to completion. Ah, speak softly! Look closely! The rose is now being made, and you say God is making it. Yes, you said God made this full-blown rose. Well, then, He is surely now at work on this half-blown rose. Bring on your spectroscope, your microscope! Quick, now, you chemist! Bring on your test-tubes, your acids, and alkalis, your spectroscope and X-ray. Analyze, illuminate, and magnify! Now we shall discover God. He is here at work before our eyes. What do you see, chemist? What do you see, scientist? Ah! I know what you see. My experience in the realm of matter and of Spirit tell me what you see. O thou stupendous sex force—sex—days of creation, thou Father-Mother Yahveh, thou divine male and female, thou eternal positive and negative dynamis! We now behold thee operating. Out from the chemicalizing mass of God's creative compounds, out of the quivering, vibrating substance, slowly comes forth the rose. But are you sure it is a rose? Hold a moment. What is a rose? Of what material is it formed? Ah! the chemist speaks —he of the crucibles and test-tubes and acids ! Hear the chemist !

He says, "The rose is made from the universal substance," or "The rose is universal substance, in a certain rate of activity." Thanks! Blessed be the chemist! Universal—one verse—one substance—no other substance—God is the rose, or the smile we call a rose—God is again manifested in the great Eternal IT, for which there is no other name.

> "Acids and alkalis acting,
>   Proceeding and acting again,
> Operating, transmuting, fomenting,
>   In throes and spasms of pain—
> Uniting, reacting, atoning,
>   Like souls passing under the rod—
> Some people call it Chemistry,
>   Others call it GOD."

Job did not say, "I see the thoughts of God," nor did he say, "I can fathom the mind of God." The plan cannot be seen ; but that which is planned—a planet—can be seen. One may see the substance of God without understanding the mind of God.

Let us hear Emerson on this stupendous, glorious theme :

> "The great idea baffles wit;
> Language falters under it;
> It leaves the learned in the lurch—
> Nor art, nor power, nor toil can find

The measure of the Eternal Mind,
Nor hymn, nor prayer, nor church."

O thou ever-present Divine Mind and Substance! We now fully realize our oneness with thee, and bathe and revel in thy glory. The mighty Angel of Reality has torn the veil of illusion, and we see the celestial City of Truth with wide-open gates and the white light of Eternal Love forever upon its streets.

O thou, in the shadow of sickness and trial, "Take up thy bed and walk; thy sins be forgiven thee."

ALCHEMY, BIOCHEMISTRY, WIRELESS TELEGRAPHY AND MENTAL HEALING

Behind chemical phenomena,
"Standeth God within the shadow,
Keeping watch above His own."

Biologists and physiologists have searched long and patiently for a solution of the mystery of the differentiation of material forms.

The writer does not believe there is any such thing as an element different from the universal substance in its last analysis, but that so-called "elements" are different rates of motion, or vibration of one substance. No ordinary test can detect any difference in the ovum of fish, reptile, animal, bird, or man. The same mineral salts, the same kind of oil, albumen, fibrin, sugar and carbon is found, not only in the egg or germ of all forms of life, but in the substance or tissues of the bodies of all the varied expressions of materiality. The answer to this "Riddle of the Sphinx" is found where Bio, or life, Chemistry merges into alchemy, over the door of which is written, "It is finished"—"Let there be light."

Professor Loeb says: "The ultimate source of living matter is mineral." To the Biochemist the above is atruism. There is no such thing as inert, or dead, matter, All is life.

The base of manifestation is mineral. Out of the dust, ashes, or minerals of the earth, physical man is made.

The twelve mineral salts are the basis of every visible form, animal or vegetable. No two different forms have exactly the same combination of the minerals, but all have the same minerals. These minerals, inorganic salts, are the twelve gates of precious stones described by John in his vision.

When the Divine Word speaks the mineral atoms, or molecules, of its body into a certain formula or combination, a germ or egg, which is the basis or nucleus of the form to be manifested, materializes. This little plexus of intelligent atoms then commences to attract to its centre by the law of chemical affinity, which is only another way of saying God in action, other atoms known as oxygen, hydrogen, nitrogen, etc., and thus materializes them, until the building is completed according to the plan of the architect or designer. Thus the Word, operating through chemistry, is the Alpha and Omega.

There would be no eagle, fish, horse, or man without the Word, Divine Wisdom, and there would certainly be no Word if there was no substance to obey the Word, and likewise there would be no substance if there was no law of chemical affinity, or action and reaction, whereby the operation of materialization and dematerialization may be carried on.

It will be demonstrated in the near future that so-called nitrogen is mineral in solution, or ultimate potency, which explains the reason why nitrogen enriches the soil.

The Atmospheric Product Company at Niagara Falls, whose promoters extract and precipitate nitrogen from the aerial elements by electrical process, are the forerunners of machines that will manufacture food and clothing direct from air, and also produce heat or cold as needed by different rates of vibration of the substance, body of God, everywhere present. The Boston American's leading editorial in an issue the latter part of May, 1918, said:

"According to Mr. Kebler, who is one of the Government's good workers in the field of science, there are, in the air that surrounds our planet, about 400 TRILLION tons of nitrogen.

That is a good deal of nitrogen. Multiply the 400 trillion tons by a hundred dollars, which would be a cheap price for a ton, and you see that much wealth is floating around in the air.

Nitrogen is extracted from the air by the use of electricity, and all intelligent Governments are at work getting it out.

There is plenty for all. You cannot exhaust the supply of nitrogen in the air—as you might exhaust coal in the beds, or oil in the wells.

After the nitrogen is used by human beings, animals or plants, it is released and goes back into the atmosphere again.

And you cannot exhaust, either, the power that produces the electricity that takes nitrogen out of the air and gives it back to man for his fertilizing servant.

The electric power is supplied by waterfalls. After they have gone down over the cataracts and created their electric force, the sun lifts them up into the air again in clouds from the ocean, and they fall down and do the work over again.

It is as good an imitation of perpetual motion as you could care to have."

The St. Louis Post-Dispatch of August 31, 1902, contained an article under headlines as follows : "How Food May Be Made From the Air We Breathe," "The Latest Marvel of Science," "Atmospheric Food Company Incorporated at Niagara Falls."

"The interesting article in the Sunday Post-Dispatch, describing how modern invention will enable us to draw new food supplies from the air itself showed how an up-to-date newspaper keeps its readers informed on the latest scientific discoveries.

Readers of this article know that science can now produce nitric acid by burning the air by means of powerful electric arcs. The acid is made cheaper than it has heretofore been obtained by chemical action. And this cheap production means cheap nitrates. Cheap nitrates means more bushels of wheat per acre, and an increase in all kinds of nitrates. Now we can obtain these fertilizers anywhere, by setting an electric current to work. The possibilities are stupendous."

This gas nitrogen, which makes four-fifths of the atmosphere, was a puzzle to early science. It seemed dead and useless. It was looked upon merely as a filler, to prevent the more active oxygen from burning the earth up. It appears that it may yet become an exhaustless common bank, from which humanity may draw wealth for all time. The story of its exploitation is one of the fairy tales of science.

By chemistry, the court of last resort, will man come into his divine estate. He will then place the "Poles of Being," and produce vegetable or animal forms at will.

Thus the prophecy of man's dominion will be fulfilled, for he will have attained knowledge that will enable him to manufacture a psychoplasm (if I may be permitted to coin a word) from which he can bring forth all manner of vegetable or animal life.

> Let man stand upright and splendid,
>   Let woman look up from the sod—
> For the days of our bondage are ended,
>   And we are at one with God.

Intuition is information direct from the source of all knowledge, vibrating the brain cells and nerve centres of the human organism the temple, or instrument, of the living God at different rates, or tones, according to the chemical combination of physical atoms composing the organism. An alligator, a horse, a monkey, or a man being organized each on a different key, receives and expresses the infinite word according to its note, molecular arrangement, or chemical formula.

Wireless telegraphy is demonstrating the underlying principle of what the world has named intuition.

Mental or absent healing is scientifically explained in the explanation of wireless telegraphy. The same substance—air, or ether—fills the so-called space in which we exist. We (our bodies) are strung on this attenuated substance like spools on a string; it extends through us—we are permeated with it as water permeates a sponge.

When the brain cells of the mental healer are acted upon by the word or thought of the healer, they vibrate, jar or oscillate at the rate that causes an arrangement of cells that manifest or materialize the bodily functions on the plane of health. This rate of vibration, started from the sender, will produce the same rate, or jar, in the brain cells of any one attuned to the note, if they recognize the operation, for it is only through such consciousness that we become a receiver. Thus we realize the truth of the statement, "Thy faith hath made thee whole."

The sender and receiver in the Marconi system must be in the same key—that is, adjusted to sense the same jar, or vibration. When the brain of the healer and patient are in unison, through conscious understanding or agreement, cures can always be effected if the chemical constituents—molecules—are present in the organism of the patient, though dormant, negative, or out of harmonious co-ordination, by the proper jar, or thought vibration, of the healer or sender.

But if the blood of the patient is really deficient in some of the mineral or cell-salts, the phosphates, sulphates, and chlorides of iron, lime, potassium, and other inorganic substances which compose the material organism, the cure cannot take place unless the jar, or vibration, of health started by the sender so oscillates, or jars, the fluids of digestion and assimilation that these lacking elements may be set free from the food and water taken by the receiver (patient) , and thus supply the deficiency. It is these cases that baffle mental or divine healing.

Biochemistry fills the gap, offers the solution of the problem by preparing the cell-salts and proceeding directly to the work of doing that which is absolutely necessary to be done, namely, supplying the necessary chemical molecules.

The body is a storage battery, and must be supplied with the necessary chemicals, or it will not run. When this can be done by right thinking, well and good; but when a deficiency does occur, why not supply it direct by a biochemic procedure?

A child may touch a button that will start a complex machine to operating, and yet not understand the science of physics or mechanism of the machine.

So there may be many methods of starting the workmen in the system that have become dormant into action. Massage, bathing, electricity, magnetic healing, suggestion, absent treatments, concentration, affirmation, prayer, all these and many more that might be mentioned, can and often do start forces that have become dormant because some link in the chemical chain of inorganic molecules has been misplaced or thrown out of gear, but when these chemicals (man's body is a chemical formula, remember) are deficient in the blood, you can no more supply them by any of these modes of operation than you can cure hunger by them. These methods are all good in their time and place to start dormant energies, but none of them will supply deficiencies— viz., cure hunger.

So Biochemistry furnishes the key to all cures made by the old or allopathic, the homeopathic or electric schools, or by medical springs or healing through the operation of mind. There are some who heal by thought transference, others must come in contact with the patient. In either case, I hold the process is orderly and within the domain of law.

This science is in perfect harmony with the Chemistry of Life operating in each human organism, and cannot antagonize any phase of higher thought. Mind or mental cures, Christian or Divine science, suggestive therapeutics or magnetic healing, must all operate according to Divine law (Life Chemistry) , or not at all. The operation of wisdom has many names, but the chemical process is one.

END OF THE WORLD
ASTROLOGICALLY CONSIDERED
(Written in 1913)

The word "world" is derived from whirl, to wheel or turn round, to gyrate. In a broader sense, it is used to express activity. Thus we say the financial world, the labor world, the world of music, etc.

About every 2000 years the Solar System passes through one of the Signs of the Zodiac. During a period of 2000 years, ending about the year 1900, the Solar System was in the sign Pisces, the fishes, a water sign. During this time we were in the "flood that covered the whole Earth."

Water causes the appearance called refraction or illusion. Thus a straight stick appears crooked while immersed in water.

"Avoid the appearance of evil" has a scientific meaning. The word Jesus is from a Greek word meaning fish.

JESUS, JEHOVAH, JOB and other scientific formulas were never intended for pronunciation as a word, but like the chemical formula of water, H_2O, were intended to express principles.

The word fish in its last analysis, means substance from the sea. Virgin Mary means Pure Sea, or water. In the Pisces age, we had a fish god, quite naturally, and his disciples were fishermen. For 2000 years we were in a water-world age.

The fish-god walked on the water and fishermen preached his gospel. Then came navigation, Columbus, Watt, Fulton, and finally submarine navigation. For 2000 years water ruled the world. Then the Solar System swung into the air Sign-Aquarius. And now it is the airship that rains fire upon water-ships, and "Alas, alas that great city wherein were made rich all that had ships in the Sea by reason of her costliness; for in one hour is she made desolate." Rev.18-19.

Aquarius is the only human (or man) Sign of the 12 Signs or Sons (Suns) of Jacob. Jacob in Hebrew means circle. The Son (Sun) of Jacob, Dan (Daniel) means a Judge and is the Son that rules Aquarius, therefore we are now in the Judgment age. The "Day of Judgment" will last about 2000 years, or while the Solar System is in Aquarius and ruled by Dan, the Judge.

So then, statements made relative to the end of the world in a general way referred to the entrance of our Solar System into the Sign of Humanity, Aquarius or "Sign of the Son(Sun)of Man in the heavens. See Luke 21 and Matt 24. The direct reference to the real time of the end of the world (whirl or activity) of competition, interest, profit, rent and exploitation of labor, is clearly explained in Rev. 18.

The letters "B.A.B." means "Doorway to God. " "Y.L.O.N." means confusion. So Babylon means the Door to God in confusion, or the overthrow of the churches that claimed they taught the way to heaven, and that heaven is somewhere other than where the scriptures teach that it is. "The Kingdom of Heaven is within you." Your bodies are the temple of the living God."

"The Holy Ghost dwelleth in you."

The "blind leaders of the blind" have fallen into the ditch and the old mind of war and competition is being gathered together as a scroll.

Out of the chemicalizing mass of God's creative compounds, out of wars and rumors of war, out from the strange shapes and ghostly shadows that creep over the face of the earth; out from the trenches of a thousand blood-soaked battlefields where God's loosed thunder shakes the world; where vultures flap and air-ships rain fire; where Armageddon's blood reddens the "horse's bridle" and the war god wallows in the mire of the old world's life-blood, there will come forth from the crystallizing carbon of a material age the diamond of a new faith sparkling with the truths of Science and Philosophy.

The revolutionary planet, Uranus, entered the sign of the "Son of Man" Aquarius, February, 1912, to remain seven years, or until February, 1919. Some astrologers figure that Uranus will not pass from Aquarius until October, 1919.

Here is a memorandum of some of the doings of Uranus. During the French Revolution, this "Son (Sun) of Heaven," (Uranus is from the Greek meaning Heavens), was in the constellation that rules France. In 1776, Uranus was in Gemini, the ruler of the United States. Eighty-four years later, the length of time required for this planet to pass through twelve Signs—seven years in a Sign—brings it back to Gemini and then we had the Civil War.

Uranus overthrew Kings in France, then Kings on this continent, then chattel slavery.

In the year 1912, Uranus entered the Sign of Humanity, a world sign, or Sign of the whole Earth, and astrologers look for world revolution and the overthrow of all Kings, Emperors, Czars, Kaisers and tyrants and war-lords whoever and wherever they be.

Commercialism, wage slavery, child slavery, competition, the liquor traffic and the traffic in the bodies of women have received "their deadly wound" from the righteous wrath of a world-awakened conscience.

To the illumined men and women, to those who have the vision of the New Time reflected on the canvas of their consciousness, the end of the world is the prelude to the Age of Regeneration. All operations of divine wisdom are threefold. First, the Heavens declare future manifestations.

Second, these operations appear in the commercial world. Third, man realizes their ultimatum in his physical organism. And so it has come to pass that as the second act the world cataclysm, draws to its end that man sees the end of

animalism in his own body. Gluttony, drunkenness, sex per-
version and "wasting his substance" in riotous living" are all
called up to the judgment seat.

Prohibition of alcoholic drinks, food conservation, vegetari-
an propaganda and clean living comes to the fore everywhere and thus we see the end of the old world of sin and
ignorance that has dominated man for ages.

"Behold I make all things new."

Then, when the animal is conquered, "No lion shall be there
nor any ravenous beast shall walk there."

THE MARVELS OF THE TWELVE
MINERALS OF THE BODY

Science has demonstrated the intelligence of every atom that constitutes so-called matter.

The intelligence of the inorganic, or cell-salts of the blood is the crowning miracle of the wonders of the human body.

The Phosphate of Potassium (Kali Phos.), is the mineral base of all nerve fluids and therefore a deficiency in this cell salt disturbs the brain centers.

The Phosphate of Lime (Calc. Phos.), in its union with albumen, forms bone. Albumen is the organic substance and lime the mineral, which, by union, manufactures bone tissue. Nonfunctional or imperfect bone is the result of deficient lime salt.

Sodium Chloride (Nat. Mur.), absorbs and distributes water in blood and tissue.

Sodium Sulphate (Nat. Sulph), eliminates an excess of water: one molecule of Nat. Sulph. having the atomic rate of motion that eliminates, or casts out, two molecules of water. Thus the fluids of liver are kept in normal consistency.

Potassium Sulphate (Kali Sulph.), is the mineral base of oil, and when there is the proper amount of this cell-salt in the blood oil is properly distributed, and health maintained.

The Phosphate of Iron (Ferrum Phos.), molecules are carriers of oxygen through the circulation, form red blood corpuscles, and give strength to tissue that forms the sheath of nerves and walls of blood vessels.

Sulphate of Lime (Calc. Sulph.), builds the cells of the lungs and when this salt is deficient the cells become brittle, disintegrate and are thrown out, producing the condition called tuberculosis.

Phosphate of Magnesia (Mag. Phos.), is a constituent of the white fibers of nerves. A lack of proper balance of this salt causes sharp, shooting pains, cramps or imperfect heart action; these different sensations are words or dispatches from brain centers calling for reinforcements.

Space will not permit a full expose of the marvels of operation of the twelve cell-salts, but a complete story of the chemical action may be found in Dr. Carey's books on Biochemistry.

PARADOXES OF CIVILIZATION

This is an age of keen investigation, of truth-finding, and idol-breaking. He who is afraid to investigate for fear some cherished idol will be broken is not a true scientist, and not true to himself.

No length of time ever sanctified anything, and the truth alone sets free. But how shall we explain the seeming contradictions that confront us at every turn?

The inconsistencies and paradoxes in the thoughts and actions of man can be explained only on the hypothesis that one power, principle or cause does all and is all, and that so-called paradoxes are but steps in the operation of wisdom, moving in orderly procedure to the completion of certain phases of expression.

In chemistry, acids and alkalis are paradoxical; being opposite, they cause chemicalization, or fomentation, which seems to be confusion. In ancient alchemical writings, this phrase when applied to human life was called Babylon, which, when traced to its root, we find means confusion.

The world's civilization, since recorded history began, has been one chain of paradoxes. The scales of competition forever tipping cause the phenomena. The producers of food starve because they cannot buy the food they produce. The makers of clothing are in rags because they can't pay, in the coin of the realm, for the clothing they make. Prices are too high for the consumer, or too low to please the producer. If workers demand the full product of their labor, they are denounced as thugs and anarchists by those who do not produce anything. In competitive thought there appears to be many inconsistencies.

Man lays his sceptre on the stars, analyzes their substance, and then dies from the effect of acid in his blood, because he does not know what to eat. He foretells the return of a comet to an hour, but cannot tell if he himself will have la grippe next week. He can tell you the hour in the day one hundred years hence that there will be high tide at Bombay, or along the coast of Norway, but he doesn't know the cause of smallpox, and foolishly thinks the decaying organic matter or pus from a sick calf injected into the blood may somehow prevent it.

He can clothe himself in armor and dive to the ocean's floor, or travel three thousand leagues under the sea in a submarine boat, and then be killed by a street car or automobile in broad day light on the level road. He knows how to keep the chemicals properly balanced in the storage battery of his automobile, but puts alcohol, morphine and tobacco in his own body and wrecks it.

He can tell all about the moons of Jupiter, the rings of Saturn, the transit of Venus, the canals of Mars, and can talk with the man in the moon, but he knows no more about the real composition of his own blood or nerve fluid or the mysteries of digestion or assimilation or the chemical formation of bile, than a politician knows of the true science of government.

Man condemns cruelty to animals, but the slaughter house disgraces civilization, and man expects beefsteak for breakfast. He preaches humanitarianism, but the sweatshops still remain a bloody blotch on the face of humanity.

Patriots, real statesmen, humanitarians, seers, prophets, the far-seeing, self-sacrificing lovers of humanity, are derided, abused, persecuted, imprisoned, tortured, crucified, and then monuments are erected with cold chiseled marble to mark their burial place; and the poet and historian vie in singing their praises, while their features are preserved on innumerable canvasses, and their sightless eyes stare out from bronze and plaster of paris in every library, or stand sullen and silent in a niche in the Hall of Fame.

Men and women teach the everlasting truth that we are all children of one common mother and father the eternal Positive-Negative Energy from which all things proceed—and therefore members of one family—brothers and sisters in truth—but they insist upon an introduction before speaking to each other as they pass. Sons of God, and yet they must not greet each other without an introduction!

O the pity of it! O the shame! Man asserts that God is love, and then writes in a book, "the fear of God is the beginning of wisdom."

Love is altogether lovely and no one can fear it. Some people are so afraid that they will go to hell when they die that they live in hell all the time on earth. Some are so afraid of smallpox that they poison themselves with vaccine pus, which is more deadly than smallpox.

A woman will express pity and sorrow for the poor and needy, and then put a ten dollar collar on a fat, pudgy dog, and let it lead her along the street, while five orphan children are ragged and hungry in her block. Women love birds —especially on toast; they love the beautiful plumage of birds—especially on their hats.

Man declares the laws enacted by legislatures and congress are sacred. He then violates these laws, carries his case to the court of last resort, and gets the sacred laws repealed. Man declares majority should rule, but bitterly opposes the majority when contrary to his opinion.

Many persons speak of "the ignorant foreigner"—a man who probably speaks three languages correctly, while his critics can't speak their own language as well as a parrot.

The automobile driver may scorch his wagon along the street at a forty-mile clip, if he will toot a horn to warn pedestrians to flee from the wrath coming, but the man on foot is locked up in jail if he runs amuck in the street, shouting, "Get out of my way!" Men say that God is everywhere, and that the devil is everywhere, too, and then prove mathematically that two objects cannot occupy the same space at the same time.

Spiritualists say that the orthodox belief in a personal devil, one big fellow with hoofs and horns, is quite absurd and amusing, and then these reformers declare that most sickness is caused by evil spirits.

A highwayman murders a man for his money, but refuses to eat the dead man's lunch of meat because he must keep the Lenten days.

Physicians experiment with poison, and find that a certain drug will cause disease in the human body, when taken internally; and when called to prescribe for the sick, they administer the drug that causes disease, believing that two diseases are better than one.

The average man declares that woman is far superior to man in perception, intuition, and judgment in regard to social life and the welfare of the family, but he bitterly opposes the franchise for women. Man is not willing that mothers should have a vote in making laws to govern their own sons and daughters. Man seems willing to give to women everything under the sun that they don't need, from chewing gum to china vases, but refuses to give them the thing they need most—the ballot.

Our wives, mothers and sisters may perform all sorts of labor, study all the arts and sciences, own property and pay taxes, and be amenable to man-made laws; yea, a woman may go down into the dark valley, where God's creative compounds materialize in human form, and kiss the white lips of Pain before she holds a babe to her breast, but she must not have a voice in laws to govern that child.

The cry of "hard times" is always heard. People dole out nickels or pennies grudgingly for charitable purposes, or civic improvements, or good roads; but a prize fighter receives a hundred thousand dollars for hitting a fellow on the jaw, men pay five dollars for a bottle of champagne, and two dollars for a porterhouse steak; and a woman will spend forty dollars for a hat that has no more correspondence to the contour of the human body than politics has to honest government, or the co-operative commonwealth.

Men complain of unjust tariffs and taxes, call upon Heaven to witness the iniquity and dishonesty, graft, thievery and fraud of courts and law-makers, and then go meekly to the polls and vote for the same fellows over again.

Tired men and women will squeeze into crowded cars, and step on each other's toes while holding straps; but if you mention municipal or national ownership of railroads as a remedy, they say: "O, I do not bother about politics. Which team won the football game?"

Dogs are allowed to roam at will over lawns and amongst the flowers, while little boys and girls stand on the walk and read a sign board, with this strange device, "Keep off the grass!"

Man must be quiet and orderly, must not talk, or laugh in a manner that will disturb the peace of his neighbor; but dogs may bay at the moon and planets, the comet, the dog-star, the Pleiades, or any old thing; and cats may curse and swear, and rip the boards off the woodshed in an unearthly noise contest, and the poor wretch who dares to protest is called a "cruel, bad man!"

A citizen of the United States reads about the Alps, buys an alpenstock and a ticket for Europe, spends three years abroad, and incidentally spends sixteen thousand dollars. But when the Swiss peasant asks the United States citizen about Yosemite, or Shoshone, or Niagara, he is oftentimes amazed to learn that the American tourist has never worshiped at the feet of El Capitan, that he never thrilled with awe as he looked at the descent of Snake River into the awful gorge at Shoshone, nor ever bathed in the rainbow mists above tumbling Niagara.

Think of a man going to Europe to see the sights, who has

never looked down into the riven earth, where the Colorado canyon reveals Nature's carvings and colors, nor passed through the Enchanted Gateway of the Cascade Mountains, where Jupiter Olympus hurled thunderbolts in the ancient days, and dug a canal between the snow-capped mountains, Adams and Hood, and let the inland lakes flow to the Sunset Sea !

"See Columbia's scenes, then roam no more; naught else remains on earth to cultured eyes." Columbia, the "river of the west." The Nile might come from its cloudy heights and pour the water of Egypt into this mighty stream, and it would cause no ripple upon its broad expanse, nor would it increase the speed in its stately march to the sea.

The firs of Oregon and Washington and the redwoods of California equal the Cedars of Lebanon; and the pillars of salt on the shores of Palestine's Dead Sea is outdone by the dead sea on Utah's plains. Truly, the man is a paradox who explores every country on the globe, except his own. The Christian professes to believe that after the change called death of the body, his soul will be wafted to a place called-Heaven a place of beauty and eternal peace, where he will have a mansion of gold, windows of precious stones, fronting the pure waters of the River of Life, that flows from the Throne of God; but let that same Christian have a pain in his stomach, and he sends a hurry call to the nearest physician and begs him to use all his skill to keep him here in this vale of tears—here among the "beggarly elements of the world," where he may remain a "worm of the dust" a little while longer.

Mental Scientists affirm health and opulence, and then fail in business and change climate to cure nervous prostration.

Of all the negative condition—devils—the race is subject to, Fear is the greatest. We are born cowards. Our mothers feared for us before we were born. We came into earth-life with a wail of fear. All who had anything to do with us feared something evil would happen to us. They were afraid we would catch cold, or the measles, or whooping cough, or diphtheria, or die of "summer complaint." Somebody feared all the time that we would get scalded or frozen, or fall out of bed, or down stairs, or into the well.

When we were old enough to be afraid, we feared our parents, our teachers, the ministers, the dark, the devil, and even feared God, whom St. John says is Love. Later, we were afraid in business, of fire; afraid the election would start some one to tinkering with the tariff, or our blessed money system. We were afraid on land and sea, of fire and water, cold and heat, wind and hail, lightning and cyclone, earthquake and tidal wave, and yet we wonder why there are so many sick people. But the silliest of all fears is the fear of microbes.

We laugh at the elephant because it fears a mouse, but the ignorance of the elephant in that respect is pure wisdom when compared with man's fear of contagious diseases, and his senseless efforts to "stamp them out," by quarantine, disinfectants, germicides, lymphs, serums, and vaccine pus galore.

Paradoxes upon paradoxes! Yet all will cease when competition is supplanted by co-operation. So, then, to sum up, we must find the reason for competition. Man has fostered competition because he thought he was an individual. Man has turned the mighty power he possesses to every object and principle or force in the universe, except himself, the greatest miracle of all. When man focuses his divine thinking lens upon himself, he will realize that he is an epitome of unlimited Cosmic Energy. Then the "Heavens will roll together as a scroll" and reveal the Real Man as "the Lamb of God that taketh away the sins of the world."

I have seen the surface of flowing rivers changed to ice by the chemical action of cold. I have seen this crystalized water break into countless pieces by the action of heat. I have seen this grotesque, jagged army rush down the great waterways like a charge of cavalry and sweep away iron-girded bridges that an hour before had safely borne the traffic of commercialism. I have seen these huge blocks of ice beat and batter and heard their grinding crash, like the hammer of Thor at the gates of the imperial cities of civilization. I have seen the surface of human thought smooth and petrified by inaction, conservatism and respectability. Under the influence of love and wisdom, or in the presence of a great necessity, I have seen this petrification break into projectiles of dynamic thought, dominated with some new concept of life, and hurl themselves against the mailed forces of error and prejudice, until domes and citadels and towers reeled and fell.

As the blocks of ice finally melt and become one, with their primal elements, so will diversity of thought finally unite and blend by the Chemistry of Energy into one harmonious whole.

"THE NEW NAME"

"And I will write upon him the name of my God."
"And I will write upon him my NEW NAME."—Revelation.

Man struggling up to the sunlight,
    Up from the mire and clay,
Fighting through wars and jungles,
    And sometimes learning to pray—
And sometimes a king with a scepter,
    And sometimes a slave with a hod—
Some people call it Karma,
    And others call it God.

A beggar ragged and hungry,
    A prince in purple and gold,
A palace gilded and garnished,
    A cottage humble and old—
One's hopes are blighted in blooming,
    One gathers the ripened pod—
Some call it Fate or Destiny,
    And others call it God.

Glimmering waters and breakers,
    Far on the horizon's rim,
White sails and sea gulls glinting
    Away till the sight grows dim,
And shells spirit-painted with glory,
    Where seaweeds beckon and nod—
Some people call it Ocean,
    And others call it God.

Cathedrals and domes uplifting,
    Spires pointing up to the sun,

Images, altars and arches,
    Where kneeling and penance are done—
From organs grand anthems are swelling,
    Where the true and faithful plod—
Some call it Superstition,
    While others call it God.

Visions of beauty and splendor,
    Forms of a long-lost race.
Sounds and faces and voices,
    From the fourth dimension of space—
And on through the universe boundless,
    Our thoughts go lightning shod—
Some call it Imagination,
    And others call it God.

Acids and alkalis acting,
    Proceeding and acting again,
Operating, transmuting, fomenting,
    In throes and spasms of pain—
Uniting, reacting, creating,
    Like souls "passing under the rod"—
Some people call it Chemistry,
    And others call it God.

Vibration of Etheric Substance,
    Causing light through regions of Space.
A girdle of Something, enfolding
    And binding together the race—
And words without wires transmitted,
    "Ariel"-winged, spirit-sandaled and shod—
Some call it Electricity,
    And others call it God.

The touch of angel fingers
   On strings of the human soul.
Anguish and ripples of laughter
   Written across its scroll.
Chords from the holy of holies—
   From sunrise sky to the sod—
Some people call it music,
   And others call it God.

Earth redeemed and made glorious,
   Lighted by Heaven within ;
Men and angels face to face,
   With never a thought of sin—
Lion and lamb together
   In flowers that sweeten the sod—
Some of us call it Brotherhood,
   And others call it God.

And now the sixth sense is opened,
   The seventh embraces the whole,
And, clothed with the Oneness of Love,
   We reach the long-sought goal—
And in all Life's phases and changes,
   And along all the paths to be trod,
We recognize only one power—
   One present, Omnipotent God.

PART TWO

"For he that soweth to his flesh shall of the flesh reap corruption ; but he that soweth to the Spirit shall of the Spirit reap life, everlasting."

—*Galatians 6:8.*

PHYSICAL REGENERATION

The inner eye—"the eye behind the eye"—just above and attached to the pineal gland by delicate electric wires, or nerves, is called Optic Thalmus, and means "Light, or Eye of the chamber."

In the Greek, it means "The light of the World." "The Candlestick," "Wise Virgins," "The Temple Needs no light of the Sun," "If thine eye be Single, Thy Whole Body shall be Full of Light," and other texts in the New Testament refer to the single eye or Optic.

Let us now search for the oil that feeds this wonderful lamp, the All Seeing Eye.

Christ Jesus is made to say "I Am the Light of the World." The word "world" comes from "whirl," to turn as a wheel, to gyrate, etc.

The human body is a certain rate of activity, motion or whirl, i.e., world, and light of the world and the temple that needs no light of sun or moon refer to the body "Temple of God," when there is "oil in the lamp."

Error is not sanctified by age. It behooves every lover of truth to cast aside prejudice and dogma and find truth.

Until we know the meaning of the words "Jesus" and "Christ" we will not understand the bible which was written in Greek and Hebrew and translated and retranslated to suit the whims and ignorance of priests and charlatans all down through the centuries.

Constantine, a beast in human form, who murdered his mother and boiled his wife in oil, was the chief factor in the orthodox translation of the so-called King James bible.

Constantine was told by the priests of his time that there was no forgiveness of crimes like those that he was guilty of and so this Roman Emperor devised the plan of salvation in order that the blood of the innocent Jesus (or Christ) might save him from eternal damnation. An easy way out for this monster, and all the other blood-smeared tyrants, Kings, Emperors and Napoleons of finance, competition and war, from Pharaoh to the present-day rulers whose thrones and scepters lie scattered and broken along the Highway of Nations (1917).

"Here the vassal and the King, side by side, lie withering. Here the sword and scepter rust. Earth to earth and dust to dust." The word Jesus is from Ichthos, Greek for fish. The word "Christ" means a substance of oil consistency, an ointment or smear. Varnish or paints are used to preserve or save wood or paper or cloth—hence they become Saviors.

At about the age of twelve, Jesus was found in the temple arguing with the doctors or teachers. The word "doctor" is from Latin "docere," to teach.

Every month in the life of every man or woman, when the moon is in the sign that the sun was in at the birth of the individual, there is a psycho-physical seed or "Son of Man" born in the Solar Plexus or the pneumo-gastric plexus which in the ancient text was called the "House of Bread."

Bethlehem, from Beth, a house, and helm, bread. "Cast thy bread upon the waters and it shall return to thee after many days." Waters are the blood and nerve fluids of the body that carries the fish on its "Divine Journey" to regenerate, save and redeem man. Nazareth means to cook. Nazarene means cooked. Cook means to prepare. Any materialized thing is bread, Nazareth, mass, maso, or dough.Thus the Catholic Mass. Also Maso-n. It will now be made plain why the Masons and Catholics are not in agreement, for our letter N is an abreviation of the 14th letter of Hebrew Alphabet, Nun, a fish. By adding N to Maso, the riddle of cooked or prepared fish was made so plain that the priesthood strenuously objected, and thus developed friction between the church and Masonry.

The disciples were fishermen. The early Christians used a fish as their secret symbol. Money to pay taxes was taken from the mouth of a fish. Bread and fish were increased until twelve baskets full were left, etc. God prepared a fish to swallow Jonah. Jonah means dove. Dove means peace—the germ descending from the gray matter of the brain (See baptism of John) . The storm means sex desire. The life seed was thus saved. "He that is born of God cannot sin (or fall short of knowledge) for his seed (fish) remaineth in him."— John. The age of puberty is about twelve. Up to that age, a child does not understand moral responsibility. "The first born" means the first seed or fish. Pharaoh, sex desire always tries to destroy the first born. When Jesus was born in Bethlehem, he went (at the age of twelve) up the pneumo-gastric nerve which crosses the medulla oblongata at its junction with spinal cord at the head of the "River of Jordan," the marrow or nerve fluid of the spinal cord (See illustration in Physiological Charts) and enters the cerebellum, the temple. This is the temple where the moral seed argued with the purely animal cells to change their rate of vibration to moral and spiritual concept. Later this seed (Jesus) drove those who bought and sold ("Even as you and I") with a whip of thongs out of the temple. We must all give up the animal life or suffer the same fate.

Before we explain the baptism in Jordan and the christening and the crucifixion, etc., let us briefly explain Moses, Joshua, Nile, Pharaoh and the children of Israel.

Egypt means the dark lower part of the body. That part of the body below the Solar Plexus is Egypt, or the Kingdom of Earth. All above the center constitutes the Kingdom of Heaven. ("The Kingdom of Heaven is within you.") The Manger, or Bethlehem, is the center, or the balance.

Nile, Moses and Pharaoh's daughter, all refer to generation. (See overflow of Nile). It rises in the mountains of the moon. Moses means "drawn from the water." Fish are

drawn from water. "There are two fishes in our sea" —
Vaughn. See Sign of Pisces, two fishes.

"Joshua the Son of Nun." Nun is Hebrew for fish.

Moses was the physical or generative fish.

Moses' laws were on the physical plane.

Joshua means "God of Salvation," and salvation comes from
saliva or salivation. Sal is salt which Saves. "If the salt loses
its Savor" i.e. Savior, wherewith shall it be salted?" Saliva
saves the body by digesting (or preparing) the food. Saliva is
a smear or ointment, and so Joshua compares with Christ as
Moses compares with Jesus. Moses died on Mt. Nebo. Nebo
means understanding. Joshua took the place left vacant by
the death of Moses. Jesus was baptized of John in Jordan—
the fluids,Christ—substance of the spinal cord and became
"my beloved Son in whom I am well pleased." There is no J
in the Greek or Hebrew alphabets, therefore, the word
"John" IOHN means "Soul" or "fluids of the body" and not
the Ego or Spiritual Man. So when the body dies, the fluids
die—thus man loses his soul when he loses his body. To prevent the loss of soul and flesh is the mission of the Son, or
Seed, of God, or the Son of man. There are two very small
nerves that extend up from the Sacral Plexus on each side of
the spinal cord and cross at the base of the brain and unite
the Medulla oblongata. These nerves or delicate wires are
called Adi and Pingali. After the seed or fish has been
Christed if it is retained and not wasted in sexual desire, it
goes up to "Galgotha" the place of the skull" and crosses the
wires, then remains three days in the tomb or the three
chambers of the Pineal gland, then it enters the optic, or
third eye, and "giveth light to all that are in the house," that
is the beth or body, all the twelve functions represented by
the twelve disciples—the twelve signs of the Zodiac.

But the question will be asked What or where is the source
or origin of this seed or redeeming Son? We answer: "Ether,
Spirit or God." Names mean nothing.

Esse, Universal intelligence, or It may be used. It breathes into man the breath of life. This elixir is carried through lungs into arteries, or air carriers, where it unites with the inorganic cell-salts, materializes (cooked) and forms granules, and is then deposited as flesh and bone.

The study of Astrology, Biology and Biochemistry, added to Physiology, will lead one into the great Alchemical laboratory of the "Fearfully and wonderfully made" human temple —the temple made without sound of saw or hammer. Before the Neophyte can fully realize the power of the Divine Eye within his own brain, he must understand the meaning of Or especially in its relation to Word and Jordan. Jordan (not Jordan) is the word in the original text. I is from Iod— the 10th letter of Hebrew Alphabet, and means "hand" or that which creates. Or is gold, not metal, but the "precious substance"—the seed. Dan is Hebrew for Judge, therefore the Creative Power operating through the precious substance produces Judgment, or the man of good judgment.

The upper brain is the reservoir of this Or and is the gray matter or "Precious Ointment" or Christ.

"In the beginning was the Word and the Word was God. All things were (or is) created by it" etc., etc.

The "Lost Word" is a symbol of the generative or animal thought eating the fruit of the Tree of Life—thus destroying or losing the gold, "or," of the body.

Hiram means "high born," or the seed destined to reach the pineal gland and "Single Eye."

Tyre means a rock. By the conservation and transmutation of the sex substance the pineal gland becomes firm and hard and is, in the fable, called rock (Tyre). "The wise man built his house, Beth or body, upon a rock." So here we have the explanation of Hiram Abiff. Abiff is derived from the word Abid—month.

Hiram Abiff (there are some who will understand) was resurrected during the delay caused by searching for his body:

in other words 28 ½ days passed (a month) and another seed was born which the candidate for initiation is admonished not to slay.

The upper brain is the Word and it furnishes all that man contains, or is. Jesus was not a Savior until he was Christed of Iohn in the Jordan. Then he became the "Beloved Son."

Why was the baptism necessary? Because there are two fish, one was Jesus the Carpenter, the man. The other, the Christed Jesus, the Son of God. The Christ substance gave the electric or magnetic power to the seed to cross the nerves at Galgotha without disintegrating or dying.

To crucify, means to add to or increase a thousand fold. When electric wires are crossed, they set on fire all inflammable substances near them. When the Christed seed crossed the nerve at Galgotha, the vail of the temple was rent and there was an earthquake, and the dead came forth, i.e. the generative cells of the body were quickened or regenerated.

The crucifixion or crossing of the life-seed gives power to vibrate the pineal gland at a rate that causes the "light of the chamber" to fill the "whole body with light" and send its vibration out along the optic nerve to the physical eye and thus heal the blind.

Let us hark back to the Nile : Pharaoh means a ruler or a tyrant or sex desire. Israel means blood, children of Israel, molecules of the blood, but more particularly refers to the thirteen monthly seeds born in 365 days.

THIRTEEN,
THE OPERATION OF WISDOM

The number thirteen is unlucky for ignorance only.
All so-called laws of nature may be reduced to thirteen.
The origin of words and their application vary widely. Thus the origin of twelve is circle or completeness, or without break or sin; that is complete. All operations that produce something may be called twelve, being complete in order to produce, the product is therefore thirteen. Thus all machines or factories symbol twelve and the product thirteen.

THE ZODIAC

There are twelve constellations, the central suns of which constitute the signs of the Zodiac.
One sign rises every two hours, or so appears to our sense, because the rotation of earth causes the phenomenon, and the earth, or sun, makes thirteen.

THE HUMAN BODY

There are twelve functions of the human body and the seed, or psycho-physical germ, born in the solar plexus every 28½. days makes thirteen. So then there are thirteen moons in 365 days. The pneumo gastric nerve, vagus nerve, that comes down from cerebellum across (a cross) the medulla oblonga-ta branches out at the lungs (pneumo) and at the stomach (gastric), and is called "The Tree of Life" (thirteen letters), also pneumo gastric (thirteen letters) .
There are twelve mineral salts in the blood and blood it-self—the product thirteen.

DAVID'S THIRTEEN SONS

1st Chr., 14th ch., 3d ver. "And David took more wives and concubines at Jerusalem; and David begat more sons and daughters."
Here follows the names of thirteen children.

THIRTEEN CHILDREN OF JACOB

The 29th and 30th chapters of Genesis record the birth of eleven sons and one daughter, Leah. The 35th chapter records the birth of Benjamin, the 12th son and 13th child.
Jacob, in Hebrew, is circle, or to follow after, also represented in Hebrew symbology by a circle of men, each one with hand holding the heel of the one in front, and thus describing a circle.
The origin of the allegory is founded in the rotation of earth and the apparent rising of one of the Signs of the Zodiac every two hours, making twelve, and the earth itself thirteen.
The esoteric meaning is based in the marvelous operation of the wonderfully made human body. All of the parables, fables or allegories of the human organism are related to 13.
Moses, Joshua, Jesus, Christ and all the characters of the scriptures are symbols of the psycho-physical seed that is born in, or out of the solar "manger" in the center of the body, fed by the delicate nerves that branch from the "Straight and narrow way"—the pneumo-gastric nerve (or vagus nerve), so-called because there are so many wandering branch nerves called the branches of the "Tree of Life."
Out of this receptacle or manger a seed is born every 28½ days, or thirteen every 365 days. The birth ("first born" —or born first), occurs in the life of each male or female, when the moon enters the sign, each month, that the sun was in at the birth of the individual.

Twelve symbols a circle, in Hebrew, meaning complete. The product of twelve is thirteen. Gallilee is a circle. The Sea of Gallilee, circle of water, or fluid, hence circulation of the blood and fluids of the body. So Jacob may be applied to the body.

Rachael means Ewe, or Mary, Eve or the manger (solar plexus) where Mary and Jesus were found. There is no U in the Hebrew alphabet, hence no double U. So V is the letter, or double V—hence EVE or EVVE—i.e. Rachael. The solar plexus is symboled by many names in the Bible, all female, whether they refer to a man or a woman, because it gives birth to the seed. This wondrous redeeming seed is exactly the same in male and female and plays no part in generation, but is the "Plan of Salvation" whereby the child "born in sin" maybe redeemed and saved. Thus, "In my Kingdom (regeneration) there is no marrying," etc.

For key to Benjamin, the 13th, the entire chapter, Genesis 35th, should be studied carefully in the light of the new revelations.

Sixth verse, 35th chapter: "So Jacob came to Luz, the same is Bethel" (or Bethlehem), house of bread, the solar plexus. "He built there an altar (same as "manger" or plexus,—womb) and called the place "El-beth-el," (God's house of God) because there God was revealed, etc.

Sixteenth verse: "And they journeyed from Bethel and there was some distance to come to Eprath (fruit, posterity, Bethlehem, seed).

Here Rachael "had hard labor" and gave birth to Ben-oni and died. Ben-oni means "child of my sorrow," but Jacob called him Ben-Ja-min, "Son of my right hand."

Sixteenth to twentieth verse: "And Rachael died and was buried in the way to Ephrath (the same is Bethlehem). "And Jacob set up a pillar upon her grave; "The same is the pillar of Rachael's grave unto this day." The solar plexus, chamber or manger is the pillar.

The death of Rachel, the mother, simply means that thirteen completes the number of seeds born during the thirteen moon months.

Great latitude must be given to writers of parables, fables and allegories.

Genesis, 35th chapter, 10th verse: "And God said unto him, thy name is Jacob (the circle), thy name shall not be called any more Jacob, but Israel shall be thy name."

Israel here clearly points to the seeds, thirteen every twelve months, that cross Jordan. Twelfth verse, 35th chapter: "And to thy seed after thee will I give the land."

Jacob (circle) means complete operation; and thirteen the seed, Israel, the product.

JOSHUA AND JERICHO

In the book of Joshua (Son of Nun), a fish—born in the solar plexus thirteen times in 365 days, it is recorded that the host marched around the walls of Jericho once daily for six days and seven times on the seventh—thirteen.

Jericho, lately captured by the British troops, 1917, is situated thirteen miles outside the walls of Jerusalem.

JESUS AND THE TWELVE DISCIPLES

Before the crucifixion of Jesus, the seed, fish, there were twelve Disciples or workers and Jesus was the thirteenth. After the crucifixion, which means to increase in power, (note the increase in power of the electric current when the wires are crossed), Paul was added to the twelve Apostles. Paul is made to say: "I was born out of time."

The meaning of Paul is small or the "still small voice," as P is from the Hebrew letter Pe, to speak, or the mouth. S is from the 21st letter of the Hebrew alphabet, Schin, meaning falling short of completeness as there are 22 letters in the

Hebrew alphabet. So the allegory makes the allegorical character Saul before conversion, or regeneration, and Paul, the preacher, after the transmutation.

Smith's Bible Dictionary admits that there are no dates to the so-called Epistles of Paul. Neither are there dates to any of the writings—scriptures—gathered by the Council of Nicae under the Pagan Emperor, Constantine. No one knows when they were written.

THE UNITED STATES AND THIRTEEN

The thirteenth degree of the Zodiacal Sign Cancer was rising July 4th, 1776, when the Declaration of Independence was signed. Cancer represents the breast and is therefore the mother sign, or woman. M is from Mem, the thirteen letter of the Hebrew alphabet, and means woman. The United States plays the part of mother to all peoples and gathers them under her protecting care. We commenced our individuality as a nation with thirteen states.

In 1782 the obverse side of the United States Seal was made and contained thirteen stars, thirteen stripes, and an eagle with a quiver containing thirteen arrowheads in one tallon and an olive branch with thirteen leaves in the other. And the motto "E pluribus unum" contains thirteen letters.

About this time, 1782, an unknown man appeared in Philadelphia and offered the drawing of a seal (see cut) which he suggested be added as the reverse side. This man declared that the seal would be adopted in the Year 1921, the digits of which equal thirteen, and that the eagle would no more be used.

Strange to say the stranger's seal was adopted, but has not come into prominence until within the past three or four years.

The reverse side of the United States Seal, as shown in the

cut, shows part of the pyramid of Egypt, the base of which covers thirteen acres.

There are thirteen steps or terraces. The motto over the pyramid, "Annuit Coeptis," contains thirteen letters and is Latin for "Prosper us in our undertaking."

Our solar system has passed out of the water sign Pisces, and thus occurred "the end of the world" —thirteen letters. So our great fleet of planets and flag ship Sun is now in the air or spiritual sign Aquarius.

In the allegory of the suns or sons of Jacob (see Genesis 29), the fifth son born was Dan, a judge, thus Daniel— "Judge appointed by God," as El is face of God in Hebrew. The first son or sun was Reuben or Libra, the loins, therefore the fifth would be the legs, or Aquarius, sign of man, where the solar system is now and where it will remain for over 2000 years.

Day means an indefinite period of time—thus we say Napoleon's day or Lincoln's day. Therefore, it is plain to be seen that we are now in the "Day of Judgment," thirteen letters.

And once more : Now amid the smoke and fire, the roar of guns and stabs of the submarine; now while thrones crumble and towers fall; now while Armageddon's battle blood fills a thousand miles of trenches and the thrones and scepters lie scattered and crushed along the highway of nations, there sits in the presidential chair of America, whose emblem of flaming stripes and blazing stars is leading the world up to the sun-crowned peaks of Brotherhood, the most remarkable man of all time, WOODROW WILSON and the number of letters in the immortal name is THIRTEEN. And so it shall come to pass, on the morrow, that America will sit at the "Peace Table" and then head the procession of nations redeemed and march on to the Promised Land of the New Order sandaled with righteousness and crowned with victory and rejoicing. So be it.

(The above was written in March, 1918.)

DANIEL IN THE LIONS' DEN

The word Dan, in Hebrew, means a judge. Dan*iel*, judgment or God's judge. El or iel, in Hebrew, represents the supreme ruler or God. God and good are synonymous, i.e. Daniel—good judgment or wisdom.

The word Darius, traced to its root, simply means an office, same as Presidency, and whoever fills the office is for the time called Darius.

Medes is from media, the middle, and is represented in the body by solar plexus.

Persia, the East, Persians, people of the East.

In scripture allegories East always means the back; West, the front; North—up, or the head; South, down—the feet.

There is a wide difference between the original meaning of a word and the multiple applications of a word. For instance, lamb, dove, hog, wolf, eagle and names of all birds and animals represent ideas or principles that have been applied to different species of animal forms on the hypothesis that these names fitted some peculiar trait or habit of the animal or reptile to which they gave the appelation.

Lion means strength and is used to designate the "King of beasts" or animals. The part of the human body below the solar plexus is referred to in the Scriptures (physiological writings) as Kingdom of Earth, hades, lower Egypt and the seat of sex desire (Pharaoh) or the animal passions, appetites, etc.

Ani: breath or soul.

Mal: bad, or imperfect, hence malformation, malnutrition, bad breath or soul (unregenerated substance), or the Ani*mal* man.

The "Lion's Den" is used in the fable to typify the animal functions that were regenerated by wisdom or good judgment—Daniel.

The following definitions will assist the reader to more fully realize the esoteric meaning of words in scripture :

DANIEL—Judgment.

BELSHAZZAR—Bel, Belial or Be-elzebub, has formed a king.

BELTESHAZZAR—A maintainer or Prince . (This title was given to Daniel after his regeneration as shown by the letter T from Tav, the 22nd letter of the Hebrew alphabet meaning cross, where the redeemer (seed) is crucified. "There is no name under heaven whereby ye may be saved except Jesus, the seed, Christ-ed and crucified."

NEBUCHADNEZZAR—From Nebo—understanding. A protector against misfortune.

ELAM—Unlimited duration.

A-BEDNEGO—Servant of Nego, i.e. understanding.

MESHACH—Guests of Sha, the Son-god.

SHADRACH—Royal or rejoicing in the way.

(Thus it is made clear why Shadrach, Meshach and A-bednego were not consumed in the fiery furnace. They are principles, eternal verities that are not affected by physical expressions and can, therefore, complete the initiation of the Ego).

In the 8th chapter of Daniel, verses 1 and 2, we find the words "Shushan the palace which is in the province (or country) of Elam; and I was by the river Ulai."

ELAM—Eternity.

SHUSHAN—From Susanna, a lily (known as the Capitol of Elam), real meaning, the product of divine mind.

ULAI—From Hebrew Pehlvi, meaning pure water.

Daniel was "By the river Ulai." Ulai here refers to the spinal cord. The marrow, or oil, in this channel is pure crystal in color.

"And he showed me a river of water of life, bright as crystal, proceeding out of the throne of God and the Lamb, in the midst of the street thereof. And on this side of the river and on that was the Tree of Life bearing twelve manner of fruits yielding its fruit every month; and the leaves of the tree were for the healing of the nations."

Month is from Moon (Moonth) and there are thirteen moons in the Solar year.

Leaves are effects of a tree.

The monthly seed (fruit) when saved, not "eaten," heals disease and sin.

"Moses lifted up the serpent in the wilderness," the body.

Moses, the first born, the seed, desired to regenerate the blood and lead it to the promised land, thus he lifted up the animal forces, sex desire, here symboled as the serpent (see the temptation of Adam and Eve) ... So shall the "Son, or Seed, of Man be lifted up," etc., etc. —that is put on the cross in order to reach the pineal gland.

"If I be lifted up, I will draw all men unto me." I will draw all other seed unto me. Study the etymology of "men." Also read "The tree in the midst of the garden bore fruit every month and its leaves were healing."

The Commandment to not eat of the fruit of this tree was not (is not) heeded by the race and death is the result.

The serpent said "Eat, thou shalt not die," but sex desire was a liar from the beginning.

A noted Professor of Greek in one of our universities says that the translation of many New Testament texts from Greek are radically wrong. For instance, "He that saveth his life shall lose it, and he that loseth his life, for my sake, shall find it," should read: "He that saveth his seed—life—shall loosen it (set it free), and he that loosens it, shall find it," which means that this "Bread cast upon the waters" shall redeem him. Gallilee means a circle of water—the fluids of the body.

Jesus walking on the water is a symbol of the seed, or fish, on its journey. Peter, from petra (stone) is a symbol of physical or material thought which was rescued by the fish, Savior.

The Optic Thalmus, or light in the room, is called "The Lamb of God that taketh away the sins of the world." The Hebrew letters Lamed, Aleph, Mem and Beth form the word Lamb, meaning innocence or purity.

Sin is from the Hebrew letter Schin, meaning to fall short of knowledge. Sin does not mean wrong or crime, but one may commit a crime or do wrong through lack of knowledge. Paul said: "I die daily" ... I am the chief of sinners."

Revelations: "And the lamp thereof is the Lamb." The word a Lamb" ends with B, which means a house or body of some kind. Now, the optic or central single eye is a body, like the outer eye ball, therefore, a beth. This is called lamb by the ancient poet.

Lamp ending with P, which means speech or sending forth or radiating, is from Pe, the 17th letter of the Hebrew alphabet, and was used to express light or knowledge emanating or going forth from this eye or "Lamb of God."

"As a man thinketh in his heart, so is he."

The cerebellum is heart-shaped, and in the Greek is known as the heart. The organ that divides blood was called the "Dividing Pump." The seat of thought is the Cerebellum. Our thoughts shape our lives. If we think continually below the solar plexus in the Kingdom of Earth; if we dwell in thoughts of material pleasures, we become animal and materialistic. If we really desire the Kingdom of Heaven, we must think of the process that will enable us to realize it.

When Jesus was born, they put him in "swaddling clothes." Now the psychic germ (fish) is composed of the concentrated essence of life and is covered by a gossamer capsule for protection. If this swaddling cloth is broken, the "precious ointment" is lost, i.e. it disintegrates and corrupts the blood.

In order to save this germ of life, man must remember that as a man thinketh, so is he. While men must abstain entirely from sexual contact, he must also realize that "He who looketh on a woman to lust after her, hath committed adultery with her in his heart."

By constant prayer do we attain the Kingdom, for Jesus said "With man it is impossible; but with God all things are possible."

Envy, hatred, ambition, covetousness, will destroy the capsule that contains the seed and thus corrupt the blood, as surely as sexual contact. Alcohol in all its deceptive forms is the arch foe to this life-seed and seeks by every means known to the enemy of man to destroy it. "No drunkard shall inherit the Kingdom of Heaven" because alcohol destroys the redeeming substance that enables man to understand or think in his heart the thoughts of the Spirit. Alcohol cuts the capsule that holds the Esse born every month in Bethlehem. Alcohol eats the fruit of the tree of life.

Gluttony is another enemy to regeneration. All excess of food, all that is not burnt up in the furnace the stomach and intestinal tract, all that is not properly digested, ferments and produces acid which develops alcohol.

Auto-intoxication is common among those who overeat. Most everyone overeats.

The furnace, stomach and digestive tract becomes a distillery when the surplus food ferments, and thus becomes Babylon, the home of unclean birds and beasts which pander to carnal mind. Here we have the reason why sickness was considered Sin by the ancients. "To heal the sick and cast out devils" is the mission of the seed. "He that is born of God cannot sin, or be sick, for his seed remaineth in him." "The blood of Christ cleanseth from all sin," therefore from all disease. Here is the physiological explanation: When the Christed substance, the ointment from the river of Jordan, the oil in the spinal cord, reaches the pineal gland, it vibrates to a rate that causes new blood—the new wine. This is the blood of Christ that heals all infirmities. Unless so-called Christians repent of their sins, the doom of the church is at hand, "Mene, mene teckel upharsin" is written on the wall.

Here are the words that define a Christian: "These signs shall follow those who believe; they sall lay hands on the sick and they shall recover. They shall cast out devils and raise the dead. All the things that I do, ye shall do and greater things shall ye do."

If there be one Christian on earth today, let him stand forth and prove himself worthy. "He that overcometh, I will give to eat of the fruit of the tree of life." To overcome a habit is to cease to do it. When the earthly man is controlled by the spiritual man—the Lord God—he ceases to eat of the fruit, that is, waste it. This fruit is then carried up to the brain and "Eaten in the Father's Kingdom." "And the last enemy to be overcome is death." We overcome death by ceasing to die, and in no other way. "He that believeth in me, shall not perish." Those who die are sinners, and therefore are not Christians, for Christ Jesus was (is) without sin. "The wages of Sin is death." Repent, forsake evil, take up thy Cross, call upon the Lord and He will abundantly pardon." And the ransomed of the Lord shall return and come to Zion." When the sexual functions are used for the propagation of human bodies, there is no condemnation or sin. Motherhood is holy, pure, divine. But motherhood forced is crime.

Unwilling motherhood has created the spirit of war and murder and well-nigh destroyed the race. Sexual union for pleasure alone is the broad road that leads to death. "And there shall be no more Curse"—Revelation. The word "Curse" has no reference to an oath. Curse means friction, to grind. The statement "Then Peter began to curse and swear" ... And immediately the cock crew," when understood physiologically, fully explains the meaning of curse. Sexual commerce for the birth of children where the parents sacrifice themselves for their offsprings' sakes, or total abstinence, is written with a pen of flame on all the pages of ancient Scriptures and modern biology.

"And I saw a woman clothed with the Sun, having the Moon under her feet and twelve stars upon her head." The Sun is the "Son of Man," the product of her own body, saved and lifted up. The Moon refers to the generative life. Twelve stars are the twelve functions, typified by twelve zodiacal signs, which she has mastered through physical regeneration.

Miss Ruth Le Prade, the woman poet of the New Time, sings of the Kingdom as follows :

> "I am a woman free. My song
> Flows from my soul with pure and joyful strength.
> It shall be heard through all the noise of things—
> A song of joy where songs of joy were not.
> My sister singers, singing in the past,
> Sang songs of melody but not of joy—
> For woman's name was Sorrow, and the slave
> Is never joyful, tho he smiles.
>
> I am a woman free. Too long
> I was held captive in the dust. Too long
> My soul was surfeited with toil or ease
> And rotted as the plaything of a slave.
> I am a woman free at last,
> After the crumbling centuries of time ;
> Free to achieve and understand ;
> Free to become and live.
>
> I am a woman free. With face
> Turned toward the sun, I am advancing
> Toward love that is not lust,
> Toward work that is not pain,
> Toward home which is the world,
> Toward motherhood which is not forced,

And toward the man who also must be free.

With face turned toward the sun,
Strong and radiant-limbed,
I advance, singing,
And my song is as free
As the soul from which it flows.
I advance toward that which is, but was not ;
I, the free woman, advance singing,
And with face turned toward the sun.
Let Ignorance and Tyranny
Tremble at the sound of my feet.

"When thou prayest, enter into thy closet and pray to thy
Father in secret, and he shall reward thee openly."
The word Secret is derived from Secretions. The upper brain,
the Cerebrum, contains the secretions, gray matter, creative
or that creates, builds and supplies all the life force of the
human temple, Soul of Man's (Solomon's temple). Hence
God, the Creator, dwells in you. The cerebellum is his
throne. Prayer or desires expressed by man in the cerebellum
for righteousness is answered in the cerebrum. Thus by
prayer to God within, and in no other way, can man overcome the adversary or the "carnal mind which is at enmity
to God."
Let us now consider Virgin Mary.
Virgin, pure.
Mar-y or mare, water.
Virgin Mary, pure water. Pure Sea. Pure Ether or spirit. Fish
come out of the water. The water or fluids of the body give
birth to the seed, or fish.
The Virgin Mary is not mentioned in the Allegory after the
ascension of the Christed Jesus—the redeemed fish. Each
person, male or female, must "work out their own salvation"
All so-called sex reform that tolerates union of sexes, may be
answered by :

"There is a way that
Seemeth right to man, ……..
The end of which is death."
"In my Kingdom there is no marrying nor
    giving in marriage,
But they are as the
Angels in Heaven."

No page of the wonders of the human body the temple of the living God—is more divinely scientific than the parable that follows :

"The foolish man built his house on the sand
And the rain washed it away."
"The wise man built his house on a rock
And it stood the storms, for it was
builded upon a rock."

The Bible is a compilation of astronomical, physiological and anatomical symbols, allegories and parables.
In the technical terms of modern chemistry and physiology the above text is explained as follows : Sand and cement form rock or stone. Sand alone, without some medium—cement—is unstable, simply "shifting sand."
The Pineal gland, the dynamo that runs the organism of man, is composed of sand plus a cement, an ointment, a smear, found, as has been explained, in large quantity in the spinal cord, also to some extent, in all parts of the body. When this cement is wasted, as the Prodigal Son wasted his substance in riotous living, there being a deficiency of this precious oil, the pineal gland becomes brittle, and does not vibrate at a rate that vitalizes the blood and tissue at the health and strength rate, and the house, beth or body, falls.
In the common slang of the hour, we say: "He lacks the sand," or "grit."

The mineral salts of blood were called sand or salt by the Hebrews. The cell-salts that are found in the pineal gland are chiefly potassium phosphate, the base of the gray matter of the brain, but all of the 12 inorganic salts are represented. In Revelations, the pineal gland is called "the white stone." In Biochemistry, the phosphate of potassium is given as the birth salt of Aries people.

Those who build their house upon a rock are they who conserve the substance that unites with the sand—cell-salts— and thus form the rock upon which a body may be built that will be free from sin and sickness.

The mission of Jesus, the Christ, was to triumph over death and the grave, over matter, and transmute his body and also materialize at will. He not only succeeded in doing this, but stated most emphatically that all the things that he did, we may do also.

Did he proclaim the truth?

Answer, thou of little faith !

> "Rock of Ages, cleft for me,
> Let me hide myself in thee."

NOAH, THE ARK AND THE ANIMALS

Few theologians are there, of to-day, who insist on a literal interpretation of the biblical story of the flood, Noah and the ark.

There are known to be 1656 species of mammals; 6266 species of birds; 642 of reptiles; 20 of oxen; 27 special of goats; 48 species of antelopes; insects, fish, turtles and creeping things on land and sea innumerable. There is not a bit of geological evidence that the earth was ever totally submerged. But, going to the root of the words Noah, ark, Ararat, etc., it is quite easy to read the riddle of the allegory.

Noah is Hebrew for rest. Ararat simply means a mount or elevation. In English we say hill, mound, peak, mountain, etc. So in both Greek and Hebrew we find Nebo, Pisgah, Ararat, pinnacle of the temple, Zion, Gibeon, used to typify brain and pineal gland.

Ark, or boat, is used to symbol the seed (fish or Moses) born in the solar-plexus to be carried up through the regenerative process to the pineal gland. Moses was found in an ark and the ark of the covenant was carried by the children of Israel (see Jacob's 13 children) through the wilderness and across Jordan, where the "waters stood up at the City of Adam."

Adam means earth or sand. At the source of the spinal cord there is a body called medulla oblongata. Medulla means marrow or thick oil or ointment. This oblong body (oblongata in Latin) is a bed of mineral salts of the body and marrow. This precious oil (Christ) is received there by secretions from the cerebrum, the upper brain—the "Most High."

This oil flows down the spinal cord to the Caudia Equina, and this is a symbol of the Jordan and Dead Sea of Palestine.

Jordan means the "Descender" or oil flowing down. Witness: Dove or dive—to descend. Dove, i. e., a diver— "The Spirit of God descended like a dove, and a voice said, 'This is mySon,'" etc.

This occurred after the baptism of Jesus, the seed, in Jordan, the oil or Christ and the seed was then Christened. The children of Israel (seeds born in solar plexus) are carried up the strait ("Narrow way that leads to life eternal,") known in modern physiology as vagus, or pneumo-gastric nerve. So, then, the poetical writer of this sublime epic could truthfully say that the twelve tribes (twelve mineral salts of the blood) "Set up stones" where they crossed Jordan, for the great nerve or "strait" crosses the medulla at the head or source of the spinal cord.

The animals taken up to Ararat, the pineal gland or "Pinnacle of the temple," simply means the transmutation of animal desires and propensities by saving the ark (seed) and crucifying it at Golgotha where it Crosses Jordan in medulla, the "Place of the Skull." (See cerebellum in anatomy and physiology.)

"And I saw a woman clothed with the Sun (Son) ."

Woman the 4th Dimension.

The solar system has entered the "Sign of the Son of Man," where it will remain for over 2000 years. In astrology this sign is symboled as "The Water Bearer," while in Bible Alchemy it is represented by Dan, the fifth son of Jacob, and means "judgment," or "he that judges." Uranus, the revolutionary planet, known as the "Son of Heaven," is now in the Aquarian sign of the "Son of Man," where it will remain until March, 1919.

From these statements it is easy to realize that all that is taking place in the world to-day is but a "working out" or a summing up of all that has been taking place for centuries. The world is awakening, the old order is passing, worn-out traditions that are no longer applicable to present conditions must be replaced by new.

Radical and fundamental changes stare us in the face on all sides. Science, philosophy, religion, bodies politic and social —all are being shaken from their very foundations—to be rebuilt anew.

There is no equilibrium, no balance, no harmony, no equality, anywhere.

Nowhere do we see a better illustration of this unbalanced condition of the world than in man's attitude toward woman.

For some time, now, this viewpoint has been gradually changing and Aquarian vibrations, or, in other words, the vibratory influence of the planets, have made conditions possible for this change.

Woman is at last coming into her own.

Co-equal with man! Mighty strides toward the regeneration of the human race will now be made.

With equilibrium of forces now possible world harmony shall grow apace.

All these truths can be mathematically expressed.

Four (4) means realization—one and three (1 plus 3) equals four.

Woman or mother comes from the Hebrew word Mem-M (womb, man, water, Mary—same meaning in all).

"I saw a woman clothed with the Son, the moon (from month-menses) under her feet, viz: the monthly seed born every twenty-eight and one-half days, thirteen yearly) twelve stars on her head." She controlled the twelve functions of the body. The Son signifies "Sun" or "Son of Man," the seed or product of her own life, saved and lifted up. The Moon refers to the generative life. Twelve stars are the twelve functions, typified by the twelve zodiacal signs which she has mastered through physical regeneration.

The seed or "Son-Sun" is born in the Solar Plexus in both

man and woman every twenty-eight and one-half days. So-lar plexus, is the center of the body—the balance, or median line, and in Bible terminology means Bethlehem or manger. ("Beth" meaning house, and "lehem" meaning bread.)

The seed or "Son," born in this manger, or Bethlehem, is taken up the pneumo-gastric nerve to the base of the brain, Golgotha, or "place of the skull."

Here is the "cross," where the seed is increased in power a thousand fold, or, in other words, raised to a higher rate of vibration. This cross is made by the two very delicate nerves or wires, the Adi and Pingali.

Having been upon the cross, or having crossed over, the seed is Christed, and in the man or woman seeking to regenerate or "save," the seed is saved), it then enters the Optic Thal-mus, the eye of the chamber, which "giveth light to all that are in the house," that is, to the twelve functions that are in the body, represented by the twelve signs of the zodiac.

Woman regenerated—"clothed with the Sun"—is the Queen of Sheba, in Bible symbology, and is represented by the number seven (7).

Then woman is Queen of 7. Sheba is seven in Hebrew, and Solomon's temple (soul-of-man) is the physical body where the Queen of Sheba found so many wonders.

Queen of seven what?

Man is only three (3) dimension.

Dimension means line.

The human body as well as the universe are geometrical fig-ures, a fact which the old philosophers well knew, for they said that sound and number governed the laws of creation.

Man is proved to be a three dimensional creature by physi-ology; and woman is the fourth dimension, by the same means of proof.

In the thirty-first chapter of Jeremiah, twenty-second verse, we read: "A woman shall encompass a man."

Mathematically, a woman can encompass a man.

Man cannot encompass a woman, for he is only a three-line creature, while she is four. Therefore, four is able to encompass, or contain within its radius, three.

Woman may be represented by the square (four lines) .

Man may be represented by the triangle (three lines). Three and four do not balance, and never have. There has not been universal harmony or balance between them, for man has never considered woman his equal until very recently.

But man is "coming off his high horse," and the scales will soon balance.

All down the ages man has considered himself the "lord of all creation." The "spare rib" which he so condescendingly parted with in the so-called "beginning" unbalanced him entirely. He considered himself superior to woman and has continued to do so to the end of the world," or "whorl of activity" —the activity or manifestation of the solar system in the last or previous sign, that representing the water age.

During the water age man conquered the water—inventions pertaining to water were perfected, etc., etc.

To return to the mathematical equation of man and woman :

The three dimensions or lines of man that can be shown on a physiological chart are the creative centers of the brain, the solar plexus and the sex organs. Woman also possesses the creative centers of brain, solar plexus and sex organs; but she also possesses another, and in a way the most wonderful of all—the breast that nourishes infant man. This is the fourth dimension or line. These imaginary lines are at equal distances from each other.

Work this out for yourselves on any physiological chart and you will never forget it.

In the triangle drawn to represent man we find the eye, also. This is a well-known Masonic symbol.

Man receives this from his mother, soul, Ego or mate, the feminine principle in the cosmos—from woman's fourth dimension.

There she encompasses him—i. e., gives him of her intuition. "Male and female created He (we) them." "Let us make man."

Yes, woman is coming into her own all over the world. What could man have done in the present world crisis without the aid of woman? And magnificently glorious has been her sacrifice, her utter forgetfulness of self. And it is not men, nor arms, nor might that will win this war, but sacrifice —the highest and the holiest sacrifice of which we can conceive, the sacrifice of woman.

TRANSLATIONS OF SCRIPTURE

"He that saveth his life shall lose it," etc., etc.
—*Mark: 8th Ch., 35th v.*

The above sentence does not ring true and is not logical.

A Greek professor recently went to Oxford, England, for the sole purpose of looking into the Greek text in regard to this seeming inconsistency. (Also Luke 16:9. See below.)

The discovery was made that the letter N, (from nun, meaning a fish,) was omitted, also the letter O, and that a correct translation reads: "He that saveth his life shall loosen it," etc. The seed, in the fable, or Jesus, said: "I am the way, the truth and the life," etc. Therefore, he that saveth his life (Seed) shall loosen it so that it may enter the "Strait and narrow way," etc. This strait is the Vagus Nerve. As has already been written, "I am the bread of life." Again, "Cast thy bread upon the waters"—i. e., the strait. Cast thy bread upon the water exactly harmonizes with "Loosen it."

Luke 16:9: "And I say unto you, make unto yourselves friends of the mammon of unrighteousness; that when ye fail they may receive you into everlasting habitations."

Literally the statement would nullify all the teaching of Jesus, and it is simply amazing that the so-called Christian world has so largely ignored it. However, a few critics from the orthodox ranks, not being at all satisfied with the rendering, have tried, in various ways, to reconcile the paradox, and to that end several pamphlets may be found in the theological departments of our colleges and universities.

Here is the explanation by a Greek scholar :

"Make unto your self other friends than those who worship the mammon of unrighteousness," etc.

Accepting the New Testament error, without question accounts for the great anxiety shown by churches of all denominations to secure the financial support of the wealthy, whether they be vital Christians, in belief, or nominally so. Proof of which may be seen in the end of the world, or age, nominally dominated by so-called Christianity.

Many worshipers of the mammon of unrighteousness exhibited much more horror over the destruction of costly cathedrals by the Huns than they did at the rape of women and slaughter of children by the Germans in Belgium, or murders by the sinking of the Lusitania.

Nothing can survive this "Day of Judgment" except it be founded upon the Truth, which liveth and reigneth forevermore.

JOSHUA COMMANDS THE SUN AND MOON TO STAND STILL

In Eales' and Taber's Physiological Chart the solar plexus, a round body of tissue ganglion, may be plainly seen. Attached to this SUN (center) is a body called semi-lunar ganglion (half moon), which is attached to the vertebra and spinal cord. A median line (across the center of body) will divide these organs, half above the line, half below.

The upper halves of the sun and moon vibrate for spiritual man and the lower half for natural, or animal man.

"There is a natural and a spiritual body."—Paul.

Now Joshua, the seed, on its way to the pineal gland is made to say, "Sun, stand thou still on Gibeon."

Gibeon means a mound or elevation. So the seed (Joshua, a fish,) commands the animal vibrations of solar (sun) plexus to stand still, i. e., cease to continue to dominate the spiritual forces, "while I slay my enemies"—that is, the animal blood that predominates in carnal thought. "And thou moon in the valley of Ajalon."

Ajalon means a "valley in Bethlehem," says a Bible dictionary.

Bethlehem—the house of bread: the seed is the bread.

Whoever conquers sex desire commands the sun and moon to stand still.

Who can do this?

"With man it is impossible, but with God all things are possible."

Therefore, all can succeed by asking help from the "Most High."

A cloud of witnesses may be found to substantiate the statement made above that the sun and moon in the Joshua story refer to the solar plexus and semi-lunar ganglion.

Eph. in Hebrew is prefix to many words meaning the centre or middle. It is defined in Smith's Bible Dictionary under the name Eph-ah, as "First in order of the sons of Midian, i.e., strife or contention between Michael and Apollyon occurs in the center of the body where the animal continually fights the upper force that seeks to lift up and regenerate the animal or natural man.

Ephah also means weight (measure or balance, Libra, the scales.)

Again, E-phes-dammin, "boundary of animal blood."

"I fought with wild beasts at Ephesus."—Paul.

Ephesians are the children of Ephesus, the solar plexus, therefore the seed. Paul the still small voice, or intuition, redeeming (lifting up).

The seeds constitute Paul's Epistle to the Ephesians.

Once more: "Eph-raim is joined to his idols; let him alone."

This epigram defines the physical man, "Dead in trespass and sin"—one who cannot be awakened by reasoning with him.

THE MYSTERY OF
M. A. S. O. N. REVEALED

All symbols, allegories, parables or fables are founded in some basic principle.

The same may be said of great Epics, the book of Job, the twenty-two chapters of Revelation, or Milton's Paradise Lost.

Freemasonry is from "frea maso" to prepare, to knead, to materialize, as mixing and kneading flour, water, yeast, etc., forms bread or dough.

Mortar, made by mixing, etc., is, therefore, directly connected with the word mason in the world of art and labor.

Certain church organizations have opposed freemasonry and ostracized the members of that society very bitterly in the past. The occult reason will be briefly stated in the following :

There are twenty-two letters in the Hebrew alphabet.

The twenty-first (falling short by one of completion) is Schin, from which the word sin is derived.

S, in the English alphabet, stands for Schin in Hebrew, as the characters of the ancient alphabet are reduced to one symbol in the modern.

Tay means a cross, +

Tau is used in many instances, even in the Bible (see 119th Psalm) but it is a palpable error, because there is no U in the Hebrew.

The Bible is a symbolical script of physiology and anatomy, a complete expose of the human body, written by men in dim past ages who knew a thousand times more about the "Fearfully and wonderfully made" temple of the Sol-of-man than modern physiologists who are just now beginning to perceive that the "Holy Ghost" (whole breath) really does reside in men and women, and the statement of the oil, ointment, Christ, "Lo, I am with you always," is a physiological fact proven by the letters M. A. S. O. N.

M, or Mem, is the 13th letter of the Hebrew alphabet (also the 13th of the English alphabet) and means woman, Mary, water or mother.

A, the first letter, is Aleph, an ox, or male strength-father. S, or Sin, here indicates that the woman and man or mother and father (Adam and Eve) sinned or fell short of something.

The early Christians, before the Anti-Christ, Constantine, appeared, understood the wonderful letters. Divine wisdom, seeing that M and A had fallen short (S) devised a plan to save the M and A.

O, from Ayin, the 16th letter, represents wisdom, or the All-seeing eye (see Optic Thalmus) the eye of the chamber in physiology. This is the eye of freemasonry, the third eye. "If thine eye be single, thy whole body will be full of light." "Now mine Eye seeth thee." Job. (33 degree member).

The All-seeing eye, O, here interposes and sends his son (S. O. N.) to save and supply the deficiency caused by the act that resulted in the fall when Eve and Adam ate the fruit.

NUN (really NON) from which we get N, is Hebrew for fish, the seed that is born (first) every 28½ days, or month, when the moon is in the sign of the zodiac that the sun was in at the birth of the native.

"Joshua, the son of Nun." "Joshua, Jehoshua, orJesus"—see Smith's Bible Dictionary.

By saving this seed or fish (it has the odor of fish, from Ichthos, Greek for fish) it is "lifted up" carrying the precious ointment, and is thus Christend, and crucified, refining it.

Thus Paul said, "If Christ be not raised or crucified, then is our preaching vain."

While I am credibly informed that but few Masons really understand their own symbols, the fact remains that they use them and that these perfect characters raise bitter antagonism in the churches.

Why?

May be because the sins of men and women can be "worked out" —"Work out your own salvation" or saliva, salivation, without the aid of priest or preacher.

This great truth is now, while the solar system is in Aquarius, "The sign of the Son of Man in the heavens," being so well recognized that the people will no longer suffer O, (All-seeing eye) and N (the Redeemer) to be cut off from M. A. S. and another Sin (S) added to Mas. for men and women to "celebrate."

M. A. S. O. N.

MASS.

Let the Lost Word be restored !

GLORIA IN EXCELSIS DEO !

AS A MAN THINKETH IN HIS HEART SO IS HE

Thought is the creative power in the universe.

Universal intelligence, operating as thought, sprang forth, "Spirit-sandalled and shod," at the appointed time and in the appointed place, and Lo! the planet earth, man's sorrowful star, became manifest.

Earth is man's sorrowful star for the reason that only by means of trouble and pain does humanity learn its lessons.

Spirit, manifesting on earth, uses earth as a negative pole, in order that the personality may grow. The mineral, vegetable and animal kingdoms use earth in much the same way. The earth is one plane of manifestation.

How can a man think in his heart?

The organ that divides blood was called by the ancients "dividing pump"—not heart. The real heart is the cerebellum and was so named by the Greeks and is the seat of thought.

Madam Blavatsky says, in the Secret Doctrine, that the cerebellum contains all, being the seat of intelligence.

The thinker, the individual or "man who never dies," has his home, therefore, in the cerebellum, under the shadow of the Almighty.

Read what the writer of the 91st Psalm has to say about this: "He that dwelleth in the secret place of the Most High shall abide under the shadow of the Almighty."

Secret (secretion, oil or ointment) place of the Most High—is that place where the secretion of oil or ointment is found. In the Bible we see so many references to oil-anointing, secret, secretions, etc.

This plainly shows that the place of the Most High is the cerebrum, that portion of the anatomy of man whence comes the oil or ointment—the precious substance that fructifies the brain of man and causes it to develop ; it is that which nourishes the brain.

The abiding place of the Ego is "Under the shadow of the Almighty," since the cerebrum extends entirely over and around it.

And again the Psalmist says :

> "He will cover thee with his pinions
> and under his wings shalt thou take refuge."

The feathery convolutions which are plainly shown in the upper brain may be well compared to the feathers of a bird. The "Voice of the Silence" speaks of the Ego resting "Under the wings of the Great Bird."

The upper brain is composed of highly specialized substance. It is a reservoir of God's creative compounds. It is that God-making material—the Kingdom of Heaven wherein all is found.

"Seek ye first the Kingdom of Heaven and all things shall be added unto you."

"The Kingdom of Heaven is within you."

Heaven means "heaved up"—a high place.

The cerebrum is, then, the kingdom of heaven, for it is within us. By seeking it we draw from it the precious oil or ointment which shall nourish the brain and therefore cause it to grow and expand.

Certain parts of the brain cells are dormant. They are in a certain slow rate of motion or activity, and, therefore, answer to vibrations of their kind.

Let us suppose, for example, that little cell in the brain is composed of spirallae, spirals of nerves, seven sets of which can be seen by the trained occultist.

In a person of low development only three or four of these spirallae will be found to be active, while the man who is already working along the line of regeneration—living the life of self-sacrifice, will show five and six in active operation.

The higher and more lofty the quality of the thought, the finer or higher the vibration. Just as the vibration of the ether strikes upon the tympanum of the ear and produces sound—so are the spirallae of the brain cells operated upon by the fingers of the heavenly man, when the Kingdom is sought.

Thought, then, is a vibration, and as a man thinks so does he vibrate his brain cells.

How many people really think?

The war has done more to wake people up and set them to thinking than anything else ever could have done. It has started that process in many people—it has forced them to think.

Thought is a particular development of ideas, something 'entirely apart from the "hit-or-miss," "ramshackle" process which was supposed to be thought.

Let us begin to think; let us choose the material from which we shall build our temples—the temple of the "Living God."

The process that the average man calls thought is not consecutive thinking. God hasten the day when people will realize that all that is, has been or will be, is the result of thought.

Thought is both creative and destructive.

Not only are we making our bodies now, but we are making those which we shall wear in the future.

By the future I mean when the individual is reincarnated.

A great thinker has said: "Know this mighty fact, the soul is but the fruitage of thought tinctured and tarnished with the emotions, passions and desires of the flesh."

First, as regards the physical body. Thought selects the food by which the body is nourished. The cells of the body are being constantly destroyed and rebuilt. The purest food possible to obtain will construct a pure body. Vegetables, fruits and grains are of much finer construction than flesh, and hence can vibrate to much higher rates of motion.

Flesh is decaying animal matter and is detrimental to the highest development of man. Much meat eating thoroughly coarsens the body, and the marks of his calling are stamped on the face of the butcher.

Another example is that of a man who drinks. Alcohol brings about exactly the same results. The body cannot respond to any of the higher vibrations.

Just as surely as the note you strike on the piano must produce a certain tone, just so surely will your body answer to the same rate of vibration around it that it vibrates to in itself.

The high cost of meat during the present war has been a blessing in disguise, for it was the only means whereby people could be brought to realize that they could still live if they never ate meat. Then, after a time, they will begin to realize that they can enjoy much better health without it.

If you wished to do a fine, delicate piece of work, you would not use coarse or unwieldy instruments in doing it.

Just as true is it that the vehicle of the spirit—Solomon's Temple—must be delicately and finely constructed.

The body must be kept scrupulously clean and be given sufficient exercise.

If your body is not satisfactory to you, it is because you have indulged in thoughts that have marred its construction. It is never too late to do something toward the reconstruction and regeneration of the body.

Start NOW.

The physical man is made up of twelve divisions, i.e. bone man, muscular man, nerve man, etc. These are all constructed with a certain cell salt or mineral as a base for each man or division of the body, see "Relation of the Mineral Salts of the Blood to the Signs of the Zodiac." Also "The Biochemic System of Medicine."

Each cell of the body is a living, throbbing intelligence. Each cell actually reaches out and grasps from out the water of life—that living stream of blood that is the life of the body—just the material it needs in its construction.

"The quality of the force called into action in any kingdom determines the quality of the offspring."

You are directly responsible for each thought that occupies your brain.

The soul is the thought man and the emotional man that occupies the physical body resembles it in form and feature. We do not here refer to the Spiritual Ego.

If, then, our thoughts build our bodies, what thoughts are the cell lives of the body filled with? We must naturally see that they are, in vast numbers, filled with thoughts of fear, strife and blood. Fears of microbes, disease, poverty, the neighbors, the weather, the night air, the dark, burglars, etc., etc.

Eternal strife for wealth, position and power, for material benefits. Benefits, so-called.

All this brings about war—the cell life gorged with blood, calling for the blood of its brothers.

Is not the cause of the war clear?

Do not thoughts pollute the very air? Is it not true that our thoughts affect those around us? What about the cells that we throw off from our bodies every minute—cells that we have built and that are impregnated with our thoughts ?

What is the matter with the people in the world? For there is nothing the matter with the world itself.

Each cell, then, that we throw off from our bodies, hour by hour and day by day, bears the stamp of our thoughts upon it. These go to make up the record of our lives, which those whose eyes are opened can read. In occultism this is called the Akasic record.

118

Then each man is the recording angel.

"Like attracts like." Birds of a feather flock together." These are trite sayings.

We see, then, that the cellular construction and fineness of the tissues of the physical man is determined by the character of the thoughts we store away in them.

The prodigal son wasted his substance in riotous living. His thoughts were turned toward the indulgence of the lower passions, like the rich young man who went away sorrowful because he had many possessions. Therefore the precious substance, the oil or ointment, the elixir of life, was sold for a mess of pottage. The seed, or Christ, was not saved. If his thoughts had been pure and clean, the seed would have reached the cerebellum and would have increased in power a thousandfold. They then would have become the anointed of the Lord would have received the oil or ointment. The prodigal would then have become the son "in whom the Father was well pleased."

When the thoughts of the disciple are purified from every undesirable thought—then he becomes the son of the Master for his thought flows like a river through the consciousness of his Lord.

His body has become transfigured, for each seed has become crucified and Christed. Each cell of his body has thrown off all its impurities and has become white in the blood of the lamb, for the blood of the lamb is as a crystal stream.

The process of regeneration causes the white corpuscles of the blood to overcome the preponderance of red, or Mars corpuscles.

Therefore the flesh becomes transparent—and he manifests more and more of the Father—he is no longer man—but has become a God.

Paul says: "Now, then, are we the sons of God."

"All things I have done ye can do, and greater."

119

As we go on living the regenerative life, the time comes when we no longer respond to any law within the physical realm, for all physical matter has been cast off from the body.

"It is sown a material and is raised (because the seed has been raised—the rate of vibration has been raised) a spiritual body, and the Kingdom of Heaven has been attained.

> And now the sixth sense is opened,
>   The seventh embraces the whole,
> And, clothed with the Oneness of Love,
>   We reach the long-sought goal.
> And in all life's phases and changes,
>   And along all the paths to be trod,
> We recognize only one power—
>   One present, Omnipotent God.

HE THAT OVERCOMETH

The above sentence occurs nine times in Revelation.

To overcome a vice or habit means to cease to do it. In the Scriptures overcome is used to symbol the triumph of the Ego over sex or animal desire. It means the conquering of the carnal mind.

REVELATION 2, 7—"He that hath an ear, let him hear what the Spirit saith unto the churches; To him that overcometh will I give to eat of the tree of life, which is in the midst of the paradise of God."

REVELATION 2, 11—"He that hath an ear, let him hear what the Spirit saith unto the churches ; He that overcometh shall not be hurt of the second death."

REVELATION 2, 17—"He that hath an ear, let him hear what the Spirit saith unto the churches ; To him that overcometh will I give to eat of the hidden manna, and I will give him a white stone, and in the stone a new name written, which no man knoweth saving he that receiveth it."

REVELATION 2, 26, 27— "And he that overcometh, and keepeth my works unto the end, to him will I give power over the nations." "And he shall rule them with a rod of iron; as the vessels of a potter shall they be broken to shivers ; even as I received of my Father. And I will give him the morning star."

REVELATION 3, 5—"He that overcometh, the same shall be clothed in white raiment; and I will not blot out his name out of the book of life, but I will confess his name before my Father, and before his angels."

REVELATION 3, 12— "Him that overcometh will I make a pillar in the temple of my God, and he shall go no more out: and I will write upon him the name of my God, and the name of the city of my God, which is new Jerusalem, which cometh down out of heaven from my God: and I will write upon him my new name."

REVELATION 3, 21—"To him that overcometh will I grant to sit with me in my throne, even as I also overcame, and am set down with my Father in his throne."

REVELATION 21, 7—"He that overcometh shall inherit all things; and I will be his God, and he shall be my son."

VISION OF IMMORTALITY AND THE NEW AGE

It seemed to me that it was noon of a perfect day, and that I was wide awake. I stood upon a mountain top in Southern California and looked out to the West. I saw the clean page of the Balboa Sea and saw the white-maned horses of Neptune charge against San Pedro's seaward cliffs, only to be hurled back, but forever and aye returning, and charging again.

Far out I saw "Islands lift their fronded palms in air"—saw Santa Catalina holding up a hand from a sunken Empire, waiting for some geological palmist to read the story of an underseas nation.

The hills and crags of the delectable island were mirrored in the curling mists that rose and twisted about like things alive, and the mirage grew and spread until I fancied that the new Jerusalem was descending out of the heavens.

The Pacific Sea seemed like a smile of Infinite Love, and I heard the jubilant chorus of joyous Naiads.

In the foreground I saw the imperial City of Los Angeles, sitting on her hills of palms and olives, like Jerusalem of old, and I thought that hither might come the Queen of Sheba, as she came to King Solomon in the olden time, saying, "The half has not been told."

Eastward the Sierra Madre peaks lightly veiled their heads with mist and fleecy clouds as if to gently subdue their ineffable glory. I saw the clean trunked eucalipti, the pendant pepper boughs and the orange groves.

The desert blossomed and a commercial empire full-rounded spread out before me. From Santa Monica to San Diego broad boulevards marked the ocean beach and cliffs, castles and towers and temples were everywhere and the "Voice of the Sea" chanted the Jubilee anthem of the victory of mind. The pathway of the eagle and the airship lay parallel, and man talked to man across the spaces without wire or artificial transmitter or receiver; for the human brain had harnessed the Ether, and the telepathy of mind was regnant. Towns and cities had reached out friendly hands and altruism prevailed where selfishness had held sway. Architecture was uniform and stately. The animal instinct in man had evolved into human love and the miserable dwelling places called homes that offended aesthetic tastes in the days of poverty and competition had disappeared and in their places were Corinthian temples, frescoed, grained and gilded with gold.

I saw no locks on doors; no prisons.

In this land men and women did not hire out to another— did not sell their labor to the highest bidder, nor their souls for place, power or "distinction's worthless badge."

In this land of love and beauty there were no slaughter-houses—no stock pens.

The fruits and grains and vegetables, so bounteously yielded by Earth's breast, supplied the wants of the sons and daughters of the fair land of my vision.

I saw a race of people who worked and served for love, where co-operation had replaced competition, where love reigned instead of hate and envy.

In the land I saw, machines did the world's work, and all the people owned all the machines. They did not make machines out of flesh and blood and muscle, but from wood and iron and steel.

The people in this Arcadia knew that the "Heavens declare the glory of God" and that there is no language where their voice is not heard." These people knew that law is eternal and cannot be repealed or violated.

The products of labor in this happy land were distributed equally to all according to their needs, and there were no idle rich, no idle poor—no millionaires and no beggars.

Above the material world I saw miraged in the air Cabrillo's phantom ship, the mission at Old Town, San Luis Obispo, Soledad, Dolores, San Gabriel, Santa Barbara, San Juan Capistrano, San Carlos, San Antonio, San Miguel, Los Angeles and San Juan. I saw the conquistadores, the Indian neophytes and heard their plaintive "Ave Marias." Some were counting beads and mumbling "Hail Marys" and some were weaving baskets. I saw the priests of the old time bow and kneel and make the sign of the cross ; and in their midst, his face radiant as the sun, stood Junipero Serra, chanting "Gloria in Excelsis Deo." And then Ramona and Alessandro, hand in hand, looked down upon me and smiled as they walked along El Camino Real in the clouds.

And, from a yellow blossomed Acacia bough I heard a shuttle-throated mocking bird trilling liquid melody into the ears of Deity and I asked aloud "is not this the New Age? Am I immortal?"

And then a voice sweet as the voice of the Infinite Mother came out of the everywhere and I heard the words, "Yes, you are immortal. You stood in the rush of Divine Splendor when God said: 'Let there be Light.' You heard the morning stars chant the Epic of Creation. You saw the first procession of the constellations. You saw Orion light his clustering lamp out in the wilderness of the southern skies. You saw Arcturus rise from the unknown sea of silence and sentinel the Northern Pole. You saw the first rushing, blazing comet emerge from the awful realms of boundless space, sweep across measureless reaches of star dust, bearing upon its flaming front the glad intelligence that the rule of law is perfect: that suns, stars, systems follow the Cosmic urge and obey the Eternal Word.

You saw ancient Egypt, saw her magic, her rise, saw the pyramids built and the unnamable Sphinx sculptured to confound posterity. You saw Anthony and Cleopatra ; and you saw Egypt hide her shame in the hot sands of the Nile.

You saw the ancient Briton throw off the yoke of feudalism; saw the French revolution and saw America banner the skies with the stars and stripes.

And if, in the operation of wisdom, the time shall come when the vast fabric of creation shall rock in universal spasm and totter to its fall, if the elements shall melt in fervent heat, the last sun die and the "Heavens be gathered together as a scroll" yet thou, oh doubting one, shall stand erect, un-afraid," and

> "O'er the ruins smile,
> And light thy torch again at nature's funeral pile."

And then I heard the bugles all sing truce along the iron front of war. I saw the battle flags furled. Soldiers returned to homes, shops, the fields, the orchards and gardens. Children laughed and women loved. The headsman and hangman retired and became forgotten horrors. Grass grew over battle trenches, flowers bloomed over deserted forts, vines clambered over arsenals and dreadnaughts rusted in the harbors. Earth was baptized with the golden light of Love. With the "Eye behind the eyes" "I saw the Holy City beside the tideless sea" and I heard the angels striking all their harps of gold.

THE END

THE CHEMISTRY OF HUMAN LIFE

The Biochemic Statement of the Cause of Disease and the
Physiological and Chemical Operation of the Inorganic Salts
of the Human Organism and their Chemical Formulas

BY GEORGE W. CAREY

THE CHEMISTRY OF WISDOM

A STATEMENT OF BEING

Life is omnipotent, omniscient and omnipresent.

Being all, life must be wisdom. So, then, it follows, that all forms, appearances, and so-called matter must be life or wisdom in that form of expression.

"Ye are the salt of the earth, but if the salt have lost his savour, wherewith shall it be salted ? It is thenceforth good for nothing but to be cast out and to be trodden under the foot of men."

God made man from the dust (or mineral) of the earth. God made of one blood, all persons.

"The blood is the life."

"The life of the flesh is in the blood."

"Thou art Peter (Petra-stone or mineral), on thee will I build my church and the gates of hell shall not prevail against it."

The above words are simple statements of chemical and physiological facts.

The mineral salts of the human organism are intelligent entities, and work under divine guidance which man has designated as chemical affinity.

The molecules of iron, lime, magnesia, potash, etc., must have certain substances to work with, such as albumen, fibrin, oxygen, water, etc., or they cannot work, that is, "They have lost their savour," or substance.

The mineral salts are the base of the blood and good blood is the product of a proper balance of the dynamic molecules. Poor, or imperfect blood, is the product of a break in the molecular chain of the salts. Having "lost the savour," some of the salts are good for nothing, etc., and hence the deficiency that causes so-called disease.

A thing is valuable only as it can be used. If the salt loses its savor, where with shall it be salted?

The mineral salts may be present in the system, but we, through ignorance of nature's laws, may do that which will cause them to become of no value in the construction of the body. Not that the cell-salts themselves are changed in any way, but that the fluids of the body have become non-functional.

Science has proved that emotions of anger, fear, sorrow, etc., generate poisons in the human laboratory. Thought is the controller of the emotions. Therefore, our wrong thoughts, working through the emotions, have caused the fluids of the body to become poisoned or vitiated and thus thrown out of harmonious relation to the cell-salts, which cannot use non-functional oil, albumen, etc., in a manner to produce that harmonious condition called health.

This great chemical fact emphasizes the necessity of carefully guarding our thoughts, and makes plain the statement of Holy Writ : "As a man thinketh in his heart so is he."

Church, temple, house, etc., are derived from the Hebrew, Beth, and in the Scriptures these words are used to designate the human body. On petra, stone or mineral, the body is built.

Hell, hades, means stomach, and is derived from the fifteenth letter of the Hebrew alphabet, Samech.

Food is digested in the stomach and intestinal tract to furnish force, also to set free the mineral or cell-salts, and these remain intact and are not in any manner changed; therefore, "The gates of hell (grave or stomach) do not prevail against them."

The chemistry of the Old and New Testaments proves that the books were written by Masters.

The wisdom of the ages has produced none greater.

DISEASE NATURE'S EFFORTS TO RESTORE EQUILIBRIUM

Disease is an alarm signal, a friend who calls to inform us of danger. Disease is an effort to prevent death.

Therefore, pain and so-called disease is more than a warning; it is an effort that opposes death. The symptoms that indicate disease are calls, or dispatches, asking for the material with which the repair of bodily tissue may be made. Pains or discomforts of various functions or structure of the body are words asking for the constituent parts of blood, nerve fluids, tissue, bone, etc.

If acids cause pain, the pain is a call for a sufficient amount of alkaloid salts to counteract an acid effect and change fluids to a bland and natural state.

Healthy synovial fluid (fluids of the joints) is neither acid nor alkali, but yet contains both in combination. Should the alkaline salts become deficient in amount, for any cause, the acid at once becomes a disturbing element and hurts the nerves that pervade the membranes of the periosteum (bone cover- ing) of the internal structure of the knee, elbow or other joints of the human anatomy. This pain, or word, can not be considered bad or malignant in any sense.

All phenomena appears as a result of Divine, beneficent law, hence disease so-called is the result of the orderly procedure of that law. In all ages all men and women have been sick more or less. In all ages there have been storms, cataclysms, earthquakes and extremes of heat and cold; no one questions the wisdom that causes, guides and directs these events, then why should we question the wisdom of disease? Disease is one phase of the transmutation of matter in the procedure of regeneration.

All methods of healing are phases of the transmutation process.

When man reaches the plane of understanding (Alchemical Knowledge) he will consciously co-operate with the Divine Urge by supplying his dynamic laboratory with the mineral base of the blood (the Philosopher's Stone), and thus make blood the "Elixir of Life" as it is destined to be.

Consider Biochemistry, thou invalid, study her truths, practice her precepts and you will obtain wisdom, and realize that you are a worker in the plan of regeneration.

BIOCHEMISTRY

"THE STONE THE BUILDERS REJECTED"

"I know perfectly well my own egotism
I know my omnivorous lines,
And will not write any less,
And would fetch you, whoever you are, flush with myself."
—*Walt Whitman.*

The constituent parts of man's body are perfect principles, but the principles are not always perfectly adjusted.

The planks, bricks, or stones with which a building is to be erected are composed of perfect principles, namely, oxygen, hydrogen, carbon, lime, iron, silica, potassium, magnesia, etc. These principles or elements are eternally perfect per se, but may be endlessly diversified in combination.

The stone which the builders rejected is symbolized by the stone which the builders of the pyramid of Cheops failed to place in position on the top corner—the pyramid being five-cornered, one corner pointing upward, and representing the sense of seeing—so the builders of the science of medicine have failed to place the mineral basis of blood—the inorganic salts in their place in the human structure or fleshly pyramid.

When these mineral (stone) principles, or elements, are perfectly placed in the chemical formulae which composes the blood, the animal functions proceed in harmonious operation. When for any reason these cell-salts, stones, are deficient or negative or dormant or get misplaced, i. e., out of combination, the stone which must become the head of the corner has been rejected by the chemistry of life builders.

The human body, or pyramid, is a storage battery, and must be supplied constantly with the proper elements—chemicals—to set up motion or vibration at a rate that will pro-

135

duce what we please to call a live body. A failure to keep the storage battery supplied with the chemical base of blood causes a disturbance in the operation of the chemical action of the blood, the effect of which is called disease. To give names to these effects is the insanity of science.

The word Peter, or Petra, means "A rock." "Thou art Peter; on this rock will I build my church."

This statement, or word, represents the creative or formative principle denning the human organization. The twelve cell-salts of the body are stones, i. e., minerals, which on combination may be called a rock. These minerals, or rock, attract by chemical affinity the aerial elements, and by their union —chemical operation—the oil, albumen, fibrin, etc., which build up the human structure are formed and changed into bone and other tissue of the body, and thus build the beth, or church of God the true church of God is the body.

The alchemists of old, whom we in our blindness have imagined were religious teachers, understood the real meaning of the statements : The human body is the temple of the living God; and again, the Holy Ghost dwelleth in you, and the kingdom of heaven is within you, and Our Father, who art in heaven. A temple and a church or beth (Beth-el) mean the same. Solomon's temple is a myth, an allegory or symbol of the human body, the temple of the living God. Originally it was the soul of man's temple, or the temple for the soul. Thus we can understand how the temple is built "without the sound of saw or hammer."

The seers, scientists, and alchemists of the early centuries of the Pisces, or water age, into which the sun and solar system entered about 2200* years ago, realized that, for about that period the inhabitants of the earth—souls in flesh—would be a lost race; that, while the earth was down deep in the Pi-

* The solar system entered Aquarius, an air sign, about the year 1900. Aquarius is "the Sign of the Sun, or Son, of Man in the heavens."

136

sces air, dense and watery, the material thought would cognize from the individual concept, being so environed that the unity of being could not be realized.

A lack of the knowledge of the unity or completeness of being, or the perfection or completeness of the body, or temple of being, was symbolized by the allegory of the temple or pyramid, the capstone rejected—or not yet placed in proper position.

The mineral salts—rock foundation of the human structure have been rejected by the medical builders for 2,000 years or more, but are now, as the earth swings into the air age, or the age of Spiritual Man, being recognized as the "Head of the Corner."

Thus we see why the beautiful name, Biochemistry, has shone forth from the slowly crystallizing carbon of dead and dying isms and pathies, and now glitters like a diamond in the crown of science.

Biochemistry is the "stone the builders rejected."

FUNDAMENTAL PRINCIPLES

He are a few questions and answers that will enable the patient to grasp the fundamental principle of Biochemistry :

First. What are the remedies you use? Answer—The inorganic salts, as found in healthy human blood.

Second. What is the meaning of Biochemistry? Answer— The chemistry of life.

Third. Where are the inorganic salts found? Answer—In all nature. In the food we eat; in the earth, rock, soil, and vegetable, and especially noticeable in mineral springs.

Fourth. Then why need we take them as medicine? Answer—You need not take them as medicine. No medicine, in the common use of the word, is or can be needed; they are taken as food, to supply a deficiency.

Fifth. Why does a deficiency occur, if the food we eat contains the mineral salts? Answer—Because the digestion and assimilation sometimes fail to set them free from the organic parts of the food, so that the absorbents can take in a sufficient quantity to keep the blood properly balanced; or some extra demand has been made upon the system—overwork, physical or mental, atmospheric or electric changes, etc.— which have too rapidly consumed the vitality of the body. It is then Biochemistry comes to the rescue. The inorganic vitalizing principles of food, having been set free by chemical process, or prepared direct from the mineral base, are given as a remedy, and are taken in by the absorbents at once, not passing through the process of digestion at all, as they are ready for the blood when taken.

There is no such thing as disease, therefore, there cannot be any cure, as commonly understood. The symptoms called disease and named in Latin or Greek, so that the masses are awed and frightened by them, are not things or entities—are not something to be combatted, but are simply and only the words, the dispatches, the language nature employs in calling for that which is lacking.

Do you see the difference between something and the lack of something?

"Yes," you say, "but people die from these words, dispatches, language, as you put it." Answer—Let us illustrate: A man goes without food for three days and nights, and has pains, fevers, headache, etc., but you know he is not "possessed of something," but lacks food. You also know he will die if the food is not supplied; but the words or dispatches calling for food will not kill him, but he will die because of a lack of food. You know this, and give him food; but, if you did not know it, you would proceed, according to the old pathology, to try to cure the pain, fever, or headache with some poison. "He asked for fish, and ye gave him a serpent."

BIOCHEMISTRY
AND THE BIOCHEMIC PATHOLOGY

A shadow cannot be removed by chemicals, neither can disease be removed by poisons. There is nothing (no-thing) to be removed in either case; but there is a deficiency to be supplied. The shadow may be removed by supplying light to the space covered by the shadow.

So symptoms, called disease, disappear or cease to manifest when the food called for is furnished.

The human body is a receptacle for a storage battery, and will always run right while the chemicals are present in proper quantity and combination, as surely as an automobile will run when charged or supplied with the necessary ingredients to vibrate or cause motion.

There can be but one law of chemical operation in vegetable or animal organisms. When man understands and co-operates with that life chemistry, he will have solved the problem of physical existence.

When the arteries contain a sufficient quantity of the cell-salts, the aerial elements that form the organic portion of blood are drawn into them by chemical affinity or magnetic attraction, and precipitated or concentrated to the consistency that forms the substance known as blood.

The quality of blood depends entirely upon the chemical mineral base. If one or more of the inorganic salts are deficient in quantity, the blood will be deficient in vital or magnetic vibration and cell and tissue-building substance.

And so to supply the organism with the mineral principles that form the positive pole of blood is the natural law of cure.

Lymph and the lymphatic system is a part of the complex wonderful operation in the process of transmuting the etheric substance—aerial elements—into blood, flesh, and bone.

Biochemistry has been and is now being recognized by the most advanced thinkers the world has known.

THE CHEMISTRY
OF BLOOD AND TISSUE

The word Biochemistry is formed from bios, the Greek for life, and chemistry. Webster defines chemistry as that branch of science which treats of the composition of substances and the changes which they undergo. Therefore,Biochemistry, taken literally, means that branch of science which treats of the composition of living substances, both animal and vegetable, and of the process of their formation. But usage has given the word a somewhat different signification, and the following is a more accurate definition: That branch of science which treats of the composition of the bodies of animals and vegetables, the processes by which the various fluids and tissues are formed, the nature and cause of the abnormal conditions called disease, and the restoration of health by supplying to the body the deficient cell-salt.

The chemical composition of tissue and the various fluids have long been known, but, until Biochemistry was introduced, no practical use had been made of this knowledge in the treatment of the sick. The so-called science of medicine has no claim to the name, science. We refer to the old system that treats disease as an entity—a something, or at least caused by a something instead of a deficiency, which all will admit to be a lack of something. It is useless for those who adhere to the practice of the drug system to try to defend it. We have the testimony of many of their most noted professors and authors, that their "system of practice is responsible for more deaths than war, pestilence, and famine combined." We realize that modern surgery is an exact science. Like watch making or house building, it is purely mechanical. In anatomical exactness, and in instruments of precision, the advances in surgery during the past fifty years have been marvelous.

While the diagnosis of disease by surgeons is many times at fault, sometimes fatally so, yet their mechanical operations are beyond criticism.

Homeopaths builded better than they knew. In preparing their high potencies, they eliminated the poison contained in such drugs as aconitum and belladonna, and left only the inorganic cell-salts which supply deficiencies when correctly selected. But this subject is dealt with in the book, "The Biochemic System of Medicine," which every student of course reads.

Biochemistry is science, not experimentalism. There is no more of mystery and miracle about it than about all natural laws. The food and drink taken into the stomach and the air breathed into the lungs furnish all the materials of which the body is composed. By the juices of the stomach, pancreas and liver, the food is dissolved, and the cell-salts are taken up by the absorbents and carried to the lungs, where they unite with the aerial elements and make blood.

When we realize that there is as much matter thrown out of the body in twenty-four hours as is taken into it, we see that flesh is not formed from the food we eat.

Oil taken into the stomach can not possibly reach the tissue as oil, simply because it passes through a metamorphosis from the action of the gastric juice, bile and pancreatin.

The blood supplies the material necessary for forming every tissue and fluid in the body, and for carrying forward every process in the operation or materialization of the human form.

An analysis of the blood shows that it contains organic and inorganic matter. The organic constituents are sugar, fats and albuminous substances. The inorganic constituents are water and certain minerals commonly called cell-salts or tissue builders. Of a living human body water constitutes over seven-tenths, and cell-salts about one-twentieth, organic matter the remainder.

The writer was among the first scientists in the world to advance the theory (now a demonstrated scientific truth) that the organic portion of all vegetable and animal matter, the oil, albumen, fibrin, etc., is formed by a combination of aerial elements which make up what is known by the general term atmosphere. Food taken into the system is not changed to flesh and bone, but acts as a negative pole, as explained in the following extract from one of my lectures:

"The commonly-accepted idea that vegetation is a product of soil, that it absorbs from the earth the material that builds the structure of the plant, and that animal tissue is built up by a metamorphosis of this vegetable substance into flesh and bone, has been proven erroneous.

"Chemistry and the spectroscope prove that vegetable and animal tissue is precipitated air.

"It is well known by chemists that all manner of fruits, grains, and vegetables are produced directly from the elements in the air, and not from the soil. The earth, of course, serves as a negative pole, and furnishes the mineral salts of lime, magnesium, iron, potassium, sodium, and silica, which act as carriers of water, oil, fibrin, sugar, etc., and thus build up the plant. But the oil, sugar, albumen, etc., are formed by a precipitation of principles in the air, and not from the soil. This is a fact abundantly proven. M. Berthelot, a scientist of France, Tesla, the Austrian wizard, and our own Edison have long held that food could be produced artificially by a synthetic process from its elements. Some six or seven extracts, as well as coloring material, are now being manufactured in this manner. Madder is now made almost exclusively by this process.

Long ago I advanced the theory that animal tissue is formed from the air inhaled, and not from food. The food, of course, serves a purpose; it acts as the negative pole, as does the earth to plant and vegetable life, furnishes the inorganic salts, the workers that carry on the chemistry of life, and sets free magnetism, heat, and electric forces by disintegration and fermentation of the organic portions of the food. But air, in passing through the various avenues and complex structure of the wonderful human organism, changes, combines with the mineral salts and solidifies, until it is finally deposited as flesh and bone."

But in order to transpose air—the universal substance in which we "live, move, and have our being"—into flesh, water and the twelve salts have a special work to do. Should a deficiency occur in one or more of these workers, an abnormal condition arises.

Not until recently were the inorganic cell-salts understood and appreciated. Being little in quantity, they were supposed to be little in importance. But now it is known that the cell-salts are the vital constituents of the body, the workers, the builders, that water and organic substances are material used by these workmen to carry on the cellular operation in the human organism that underlies and forms the basis of all animal or vegetable tissue. Should a deficiency occur in one or more of these twelve workmen, abnormal conditions arise. These abnormal conditions are known by the general term disease, and accordingly as they manifest in different ways and in different parts of the body, they have been designated by various names. But these names totally fail to express the real trouble. Every disease which afflicts the human race is due to a lack of one or more of these inorganic workers. Every pain or unpleasant sensation indicates a lack of some constituent of the blood.

Having learned that disease is not a thing, not an entity, animate or inanimate, but a condition due to a lack of some inorganic constituent of the blood, it follows naturally that the proper method of cure is to supply to the blood that which is lacking.

In the treatment of disease, the use of anything not a constituent of the blood is unnecessary, and to give poison to a sick person is barbarous and inhuman. True, many have survived such treatment, but equally many have been hurried to their graves.

Biochemistry would seek to ascertain what is lacking in disease, and supply it in just the form needed.

CELLULAR PATHOLOGY

All diseases that are curable are cured in a natural manner through the circulation; the constituent parts of the human organism, which are carried by the blood vessels and transude through the walls of these "branches of the tree of life" into the surrounding tissue, restore normal conditions when the blood contains the proper amount of water, sodium, ferrum, potassium, calcium, magnesia, and silica.

Deficiencies in the cell-salts produce pains, fever, spasms, or some other cry of distress. These so-called symptoms are words, or dispatches, calling for what is needed. And when the call is for the phosphate of potassium to supply nerve cells, shall we give morphine? "He asked for bread, and ye gave him a stone."

When the call is for the phosphate of iron, in order that more oxygen may be conducted through the organism, and thereby increase vitality, shall we give alcohol? "He asked for fish and ye gave him a serpent."

It will be observed that there is nothing miraculous about the biochemic procedure—it is simply natural law.

The constituents of our bodies, planned by Infinite Intelligence, keep all parts of its wondrous mechanism in harmonious co-ordination when present in proper magnitude and amount. Harmony cannot be obtained when deficiencies exist by introducing a poison into the system.

The symptoms may be changed to those that manifest differently, but the patient is not cured.

Calomel does not cure; it simply sets up a diarrhoea in place of constipation. Opium does not cure; it sets up paralysis of nerve centres in place of neuralgia (Greek and Latin for nerve pain).

We do not claim magical curative properties for the biochemic materia medica. We only point out the law of the chemistry of life.

Is there any system of teaching or practice before the world to-day that can be said to present the law of cure as full-rounded and many-sided, clear, explicit, without evasion or ambiguity, as does the science of Biochemistry?

Let the sick bear in mind that there is but one way to be restored to health, and that is the natural way : through the blood by supplying deficiencies. It will require just as much time to cure as nature requires, working in a natural way. The food or workers called for must be supplied; calomel, aconite, belladonna, salicylic acid, opium, etc. (we do not refer to the homeopathic triturations of these drugs) are not constituent parts of blood, are not found in the human organism naturally, and, when taken into the system, set up their own vibration or action, in place of the condition naturally produced by a deficiency in the component parts of the organism, and are worse than the disease for which they are given. When a twig is broken from a branch, we know a new one will grow again to the same size, if water is supplied to the soil and conditions favorable to its growth are furnished; we do not expect to supply a new growth by legerdemain, or some short cut—say by putting an "active poison" about the roots of the tree—or injecting beneath its bark a nameless lymph wherein sport the festive bacilli and all-pervading microbes.

We realize the branch must be restored in a natural manner by the constituent parts of the tree, operating or circulating through the physiology of the tree, and thus carrying on the process of growth.

THE VIEWS OF SCIENTISTS

Professor Virchow, in his lecture on "Cellular Pathology," says (see lecture 14) "the cells of the organism are not fed, they feed themselves. The absorption of matter into the interior of the cells is an act of the cells themselves."

Alfred Binet, a noted French scientist, says, in his work, "The Psychic Life of Micro-organism"; "The micro-organisms do not nourish themselves indiscriminately, nor try to feed blindly upon every substance that chance may throw in their way. The microscopic cell in some manner knows how to choose and distinguish alimentary substances from particles of sand."

So I am led to believe that the cells are intelligent organisms and can choose their nourishment. This being the case, how foolish, if not criminal, to place only a poisonous agent within their reach.

As the researches of Binet, the French scientist, show that micro-organisms—infusoria—select their own food from the material at hand, so does the Pomeranian scientist, the great Virchow, clearly demonstrate that the cells that build the human form divine also select their nourishment from material within reach, and that nothing foreign to their constituent parts can be forced upon them—except to produce injury or death. Professor Virchow's researches demonstrate the fact that ab- normal cells are caused by a lack of the chemical constituents that are required to produce normal cells.

The renowned Dr. Schuessler says: "The inorganic substances in the blood and tissue are sufficient to heal all diseases that are curable at all. The question whether this or that dis- ease is or is not dependent on the existence of germs, fungi, or baccilli is of no importance in biochemic treatment. If the remedies are used according to the symptoms, the desired end, that of curing disease, will be gained in the shortest way. Long-standing chronic diseases, which have been brought about by overdosing or use of poisonous drugs, quinine, mercury, morphine, alcohol, etc., may be cured by minute doses of cell-salts."

Professor Liebig, the world-wide authority in chemistry, says : "It happens that a tissue in disease reaches such a degree of density, becomes so clogged, that the salt solution of the blood cannot enter to feed and nourish; but, if for therapeutic purposes, a solution of salt be so triturated and given so diluted that all its molecules are set free, it is presumable that no hindrance will be in the way of these molecules to enter the abnormally condensed part of tissue."

The body is made up of cells. Different kinds of cells build up the different tissues of the body. The difference in the cells is largely due to the different mineral salts that enter into their composition. If we burn the body, or any tissue of it, we obtain the ashes. These are the mineral or inorganic constituents of the body, the salts of iron, lime, magnesium, etc. They are the tissue builders, and both the structure and vitality of the body depend upon their proper quantity and distribution in every cell.

Professor Huxley said : "Those who are conversant with the present state of biology will hardly hesitate to admit that the conception of life of one of the higher animals as the summation of the lives of a cell aggregate, brought into harmonious relation and action by a co-ordinative machinery formed by some of these cells, constitutes a permanent acquisition to physiological science. I believe it will, in a short time, become possible to introduce into the human organism a molecular sub- stance that will by the law of chemical affinity find its way to the particular group of cells or nerve plexus that may be in need of it."

We know that the cell-salts, or mineral workers, in the blood are infinitesimally sub-divided in the food we eat. Nature works everywhere with immense numbers of infinitely small atoms, which can only be perceived by our dull organs of sense when presented to them in finite masses. The smallest image our eye can recognize is produced by billions of waves of light.

A granule of salt which we can scarcely taste contains millions and millions of groups of atoms which no human eye will ever discern. A search for the ultimate atom will surely end in complete recognition of the operation of wisdom, or Omnipresent Life.

One quart of milk is found by analysis to contain about the six-millionth of a grain of iron; a child fed on milk receives each time one milligram of iron in a half-pint of milk, which is only the fourth part of the above minute fraction of one part of a grain of iron. But this infinitesimal amount supplies the iron molecules needed to carry a full supply of oxygen to all parts of the organism.

The proportion of fluorine in the human organism is still less than that of iron.

Professor Liebig says : "Hydrochloric acid, diluted with one thousand parts of water, readily dissolves the fibrin of meat and the gluten of cereals, and this solvent power is decreased when the acid solution is made stronger." One red-blood corpuscle does not exceed the one hundred and twenty-millionth of a cubic inch. There are over three millions such cells in one droplet of blood, and these cells carry iron and other mineral workers. How necessary, then, to administer these salts in minute molecular form!

THE BIOCHEMIC PATHOLOGY
OF EXUDATIONS, SWELLINGS, ETC.

It is very important for the student of Biochemistry to fully understand the real cause of exudations, swellings, inflammation, eruptions and all accumulations of all so-called morbid matter which accompany disease.

Heteroplasm is defined by Virchow as a substance foreign to the normal constituent parts of the human organism. It must be that the normal constituent parts of the body have become abnormal for some reason, as the change occurs in the organism of man and not outside.

The fluids of the body, containing oil, fibrin and other albuminous substances, could not so combine as to render them non-functional, or to form vitiated compounds, causing exudations, eruptions, etc., if the vitalizers, the workers, called inorganic cell-salts, were present in proper quantity. There is a small amount of muriatic acid in gastric fluids, and a deficiency of the same causes indigestion and possibly catarrh of the stomach, which means exudation of certain organic matter from the blood; but this abnormal state would not exist unless there first arises a deficiency in some one or more of the inorganic or mineral salts. Muriatic acid is formed by the union of certain dissimilar substances, which conjoin and form new compounds. This is Biochemistry— that is, life chemistry, the real definition of the word.

Any breaking up of the chain of continuity of the cell-salts, of course, disturbs this process of forming new organic material to replace that cast off as worn out and useless.

Let us take a condition called acidity, or an excess of acid. It is well known that either acid or alkali alone may be injurious to man and seriously interfere with the process of life, while a proper combination of the same forms natural fluids of the body.

There is not, properly speaking, an excess of acid, but a deficiency in the alkaline cell-salts.

A deficiency of sodium phosphate causes a breaking up of the basis of certain parts of the blood plasma, which causes, or allows, the acid to stand alone and thus produce a disturbance. Of course, this is due entirely to a lack of the alkaline salts a proper balance of them—and not to an excess of acid. When the true cause of eruptions, swellings, exudations, etc., is fully understood, the names now used to designate the supposed difference will not be used.

Instead of treating a certain disease (which simply means not at ease), the physician will learn the telegraphy of the intricate, complex, marvelous human machine and know what is asked for in the words now, or heretofore, supposed to simply be pain or exudations.

CHEMICAL OPERATION

A child may touch a button that will start a complex machine to operating, and yet not understand the science of physics or the mechanism of the machine.

So many systems of healing may be the means of starting the workmen in the system that have become dormant into action. Massage, bathing, electricity, magnetic healing, suggestion, absent treatments, concentration, affirmation, prayer, all these and many more that might be mentioned, can and often do start forces that have become dormant because some link in the chemical chain of inorganic molecules has been misplaced or thrown out of gear, but when these chemicals (mans body is a chemical formula, remember) are deficient in the blood, you can no more supply them by any of these modes of operation than you can cure hunger by them. These methods are all good in their time and place to start dormant energies, but none of them will supply deficiencies—viz., cure hunger.

So Biochemistry furnishes the key to all cures made by the old or allopathic, the homoeopathic or electic schools, or by medical springs or healing through the operation of mind.

There are some who heal by thought transference, others must come in contact with the patient. In either case, I hold the process is orderly and within the domain of law.

This science is in perfect harmony with the Chemistry of Life operating in each human organism, and cannot antagonize any phase of higher thought. Mind, or mental cures, Christian or Divine science, suggestive therapeutics or magnetic healing, must all operate according to Divine law (Life Chemistry), or not at all. The operation of wisdom has many names, but the chemical process is one.

MAN'S DIVINE ESTATE

A PROPHECY OF THE AGE OF ALCHEMY

Biologists and physiologists have searched long and patiently for a solution of the mystery of the differentiation of material forms.

No ordinary test can detect any difference in the ovum of fish, reptile, animal, bird, or man. The same mineral salts, the same kind of oil, albumen, fibrin, or sugar, or carbon is found, not only in the egg or germ of all forms of life but in the substance or tissue of the bodies of all the varied expressions of materiality.

The answer to this "Riddle of the Sphinx" is found where Bio, or Life, Chemistry merges into alchemy, over the door of which is written, "It is finished"—"Let there be light."

Professor Loeb says : "The ultimate source of living matter is chemical." To the Biochemist the above is a truism. There is no such thing as inert, or dead, matter. All is life.

The base of all manifestation is mineral. Out of the dust, ashes, or minerals of the earth physical man is made.

The twelve mineral salts are the basis of every visible form, animal or vegetable. No two different forms have exactly the same combination of the minerals, but all have the same minerals.

These minerals, inorganic salts, are the twelve gates of precious stones described by John in his vision. When the Divine Word speaks the mineral atoms, or molecules, of its body into a certain formula or combination, a germ or egg, which is the basis or nucleus of the form to be manifested, materializes. This little plexus of intelligent atoms then commences to attract to its centre by the law of chemical affinity, which is only another way of saying God in action, other atoms known as oxygen, hydrogen, nitrogen, etc., and thus materializes them, until the building is completed according to the plan of the architect or designer. Thus the Word, operating through chemistry, is the Alpha and Omega.

There would be no eagle, fish, horse, or man without the Word, Divine Wisdom, and there would certainly be no Word, if there was no substance to obey the Word, and likewise there would be no substance, if there was no law of chemical affinity, or action and reaction, whereby the operation of materialization and dematerialization may be carried on.

It will be demonstrated in the near future, that so-called nitrogen is mineral in solution, or ultimate potency, which explains the reason why nitrogen enriches the soil.

The Atmospheric Product Company at Niagara Falls, whose promoters expect to extract and condense nitrogen from the aerial elements by electrical process, are the forerunners of machines that will manufacture our food and clothing direct from the air, and also produce heat or cold as needed by different rates of vibration of the substance, body of God, everywhere present.

Neither light nor heat comes from the sun, for they are not entities that can come or go. They are effects or results. The sun is surely a great dynamo, or vibrating centre of Divine Energy, which by its thought moves the atoms of our earth-envelope, and by vibration or motion chemically causes light and heat in different degrees, according to its good will and pleasure.

By chemistry, the court of last resort, will man come into his divine estate". He will then place the "Poles of Being," and produce vegetable or animal forms at will.

Thus the prophecy of man's dominion will be fulfilled, for he will have attained knowledge which will enable him to manufacture a psychoplasm (if I may be permitted to coin a word), from which he can bring forth all manner of vegetable or animal life.

Let man stand upright and splendid,
Let woman look up from the sod—
For the days of our bondage are ended,
And we are at one with God.

INTUITION, OR THE INFINITE VIBRATION

Intuition is information direct from the source of all knowledge, vibrating the brain cells and nerve centres of the human organism—the temple, or instrument, of the living God—at different rates, or tones, according to the chemical combination of physical atoms composing the organism. An alligator, a horse, a monkey, or a man, being organized each on a different key, receives and expresses the infinite word according to its note, molecular arrangement, or chemical formula.

Wireless telegraphy is demonstrating the underlying principle of what the world has named intuition.

Mental, or absent healing, is scientifically explained in the explanation of wireless telegraphy. The same substance—air, or ether—fills the so-called space in which we exist. We (our bodies) are strung on this attenuated substance like spools on a string; it extends through us—we are permeated with it as water permeates a sponge.

When the brain cells of the mental healer are acted upon by the word or thought of the healer, they vibrate, jar, or oscillate at the rate that causes an arrangement of cells that manifests or materializes the bodily functions on the plane of health. This rate of vibration, started from the sender, will produce the same rate, or jar, in the brain cells of any one attuned to the note, providing they recognize the operation, for it is only through such consciousness that we become a receiver.

Thus we realize the truth of the statement, "Thy faith hath made thee whole."

The sender and receiver in the Marconi system must be in the same key—that is, adjusted to sense the same jar, or vibration. When the brain of the healer and patient are in unison, through conscious understanding or agreement, cures can always be effected, if the chemical constituents— molecules—are present in the organism of the patient, though dormant, negative, or out of harmonious co-ordination, by the proper jar, or thought vibration, of the healer or sender.

But, if the blood of the patient is really deficient in some of the mineral salts, or cell-salts, the phosphates, sulphates, and chlorides of iron, lime, potassium, and other inorganic substances which compose the material organism, the cure cannot take place unless the jar, or vibration, of health started by the sender so oscillates, or jars, the fluids of digestion and assimilation that these lacking elements are set free from the food and water taken by the receiver (patient), and thus supply the deficiency. It is these cases that baffle mental or divine healing.

Biochemistry fills the gap, offers the solution of the problem by preparing the cell-salts and proceeding directly to the work of doing that which is absolutely necessary to be done, namely, supplying the necessary chemical molecules.

The body is a storage battery, and must be supplied with the necessary chemicals, or it will not run. When this can be done by right thinking, well and good ; but, when a deficiency does occur, why not supply it direct by a biochemic procedure ? Mental science is an incomplete science without Biochemistry.

THE SO-CALLED ELEMENTS

So far as science has been able to weigh, measure, or in any manner cognize them, there seems to be about seventy-two elements in nature, viz., in the earth, water, and air, a combination of which makes manifest all we see or recognize in the material world.

We do not print the following as an ultimatum, for certain changes in the aerial elements, as well as in the cellular structure of the human brain may, and doubtless will, enable man to penetrate deeper and deeper into the Holy of Holies of Omnipresent Life.

We do not believe there is any such thing as an element different from the "universal substance in its last analysis. We believe that so-called "elements" are different rates of motion, or vibration of one substance.

Behind all chemical phenomena,

"Standeth God within the shadow,
Keeping watch above His own."

The names and abbreviations of the so-called principles or elements are as follows :

Aluminum	Al	Copper	Cu
Antimone (Stribium)	Sb	Didymium	Di
Argon	Ar	Erbium	Er
Arsenic	As	Fluorine	F
Barnim	Ba	Glucinum	G
Bismuth	Bi	Gold (Aurum)	Au
Baron	B	Hydrogen	H
Bromine	Br	Helium	Hm
Cadmium	Cd	Indium	In
Caesium	Cs	Iodine	I
Calcium	Ca	Indium	Ir
Carbon	C	Iron (Ferrum)	Fe
Cerium	Ce	Lanthanum	La
Chlorine	Cl	Lead (Plumbum)	Pl
Chromium	Cr	Lithium	Li
Cobalt	Co	Magnesium	Mg

Manganese......................Mn	Silver (Argentum)...........Ag
Mercury (Hydrargyrum)......Hg	Sodium (Natrum)............Na
Molybdenum..................Mo	Strontium.......................Sr
Nickel............................Ni	Sulphur...........................S
Niobium........................Nf	Tantalum.......................Ta
Nitrogen.........................N	Tellerium......................Te
Osmium.........................Os	Thallium........................Tl
Oxygen...........................O	Thorium........................Th
Palladium.......................Pd	Tin (Strannum)...............Sr
Phosphorus......................P	Titanium........................Ti
Platinum........................Pt	Tungsten (Wolfram).........W
Potassium (Kalium)............K	Uranium.........................U
Radium..........................Rm	Vanadium........................V
Rhodium........................Ro	Yttrium...........................Y
Rubidium........................Rb	Zinc..............................Zn
Selenium.........................Se	Zirconium......................Zr
Silicon (Silica)..................Si	

Ten or twelve more might be added, but their atomic weight
and affinities are so uncertain that we have omitted them for
the present.

ESOTERIC CHEMISTRY

In this strenuous age of reconstruction, while God's creative compounds are forming a new race in the morning of a new age, all who desire physical regeneration should strive by every means within their reach to build new tissue, nerve fluids and brain cells, thus literally making "new bottles for the new wine." For be it known to all men that the word "wine" as used in Scripture, means blood when used in connection with man. It also means the sap of trees and juice of vegetables or fruit.

The parable of turning water into wine at the marriage at Cana in Galilee is a literal statement of a process taking place every heart beat in the human organism.

Galilee means a circle of water or fluid—the circulatory system. Cana means a dividing place—the lungs. In the Greek, "A place of reeds," or cells of lungs that vibrate sound.

Biochemists have shown that food does not form blood, but simply furnishes the mineral base by setting free the inorganic or cell-salts contained in all food stuff. The organic part, oil, fibrin, albumen, etc., contained in food is burned or digested in the stomach and intestinal tract to furnish motive power to operate the human machine and draw air into the lungs, thence into the arteries, i.e., the air carriers.

Therefore, it is clearly proven that air (spirit) unites with the minerals and forms blood, proving that the oil, albumen, etc., found in the blood, is created every breath at the "marriage in Cana of Galilee."

Air was called water or the pure sea, viz. : Virgin Mary. So we see how water is changed into wine—blood—every moment.

In the new age, we will need perfect bodies to correspond with the higher vibration, or motion of the new blood, for "old bottles (bodies) cannot contain the new wine."

Another allegorical statement typifying the same truth reads,

"And I saw a new Heaven and a new Earth," i.e., new mind and new body.

Biochemistry may well say with Walt Whitman: "To the sick lying on their backs I bring help, and to the strong, up-right man I bring more needed help." To be grouchy, cross, irritable, despondent, or easily discouraged, is prima facie evidence that the fluids of the stomach, liver and brain are not vibrating at the normal rate, the rate that results in equi-librium or health. Health cannot be qualified, i.e., poor health or good health. There must be either health or dishealth ; ease of disease. We do not say poor ease or good ease. We say ease or disease, viz., not at ease.

A sufficient amount of the cell-salts of the body, properly combined and taken as food—not simply to cure some ache, pain or exudation—forms blood that materializes in healthy fluids, flesh and bone tissue.

The microscope increases the rate of motion of the cells of the retina and we see things that were occulted to the natur-al rate of the vibration of sight cells. Increase the rate of the activity of brain cells by supplying more of the dynamic molecules of the blood, known as mineral or cell-salts of lime, potash, solium, iron, magnesia, silica, and we see men-tally, truths that we could not sense at lower or natural rates of motion, although the lower rate may manifest ordinary health.

Natural man, or natural things, must be raised from the level of nature to super-natural, in order to realize new concepts that lie, waiting for recognition, above the solar-plexus, that is, above the animal or natural man.

The postive pole of Being must be "lifted up" from the Kingdom of Earth, animal desire below the solar-plexus, to the pineal gland that connects the cerebellum, the temple of the Spiritual Ego, with the optic thalmus, the third eye.

By this regenerative process millions of dormant cells of the brain are resurrected and set in operation, and then man no longer "sees through a glass darkly," but with the Eye of Spiritual understanding.

Biochemistry is the sign-board pointing to the open country, to hills and green fields of health and the truth that shall set the seeking Ego free from poverty and disease.

THE FALLACY OF THE GERM THEORY OF DISEASE

The true physician says, with Emerison, "I will proclaim what I prove to be true to-day, though it contradict what I have advocated all my life."

Do we try to use reason in figuring out any problem ? Long ages of working for self-preservation have taught mankind that when a certain sensation is felt at the pit of the stomach it is caused by hunger and that, if food is taken, the symptom will disappear.

But the hungry one does not once think of a germ or microbe causing that gnawing sensation. He realizes, intuitively, that the human laboratory is sending out an S.O.S. to let the owner know that it needs fuel for its furnace, and that, given the fuel, combustion will at once begin and heat and energy will be furnished to run the human dynamo. At the same time, in this process of generating heat and energy, the mineral particles which are contained in the food will be set free, taken up by the absorbents and carried into the blood, the river of life, and distributed to all parts of the body.

As this wonderful river flows through, each tiny individual cell reaches out and actually selects from the stream, the inorganic cell-salt that it needs to re-build that portion of itself which has been destroyed in the continuous process of tearing down and building up.

If each cell is furnished with material to replace that which is torn down, then there is no interruption of the orderly process of nature and conesquently there is perfect equilibrium.

When we repair a house, or any article of use, we select the same kind of material that was employed in its construction. Why should not this rule hold good when applied to the "Temple of God"—the human body? When we stop to really think about it, does it not seem unreasonable and absurd to give it poisons and drugs of any kind?

No actual progress has been made in the definite cure of any disease. In surgery, however, which is mechanical in its operation, marvelous progress has been made. Take such a common disease as pneumonia, for instance ; one is never sure whether the patient will live, or die. If the symptoms do not cease, it is evident that the body has not been supplied with the proper material, else it would not be sending out signals, calling attention to itself.

If the little cells of the body, in their reaching out to grasp from the blood that which they need, do not find it, they do not take anything. What is the result when a person cannot get food ? We do not say he has "caught" hunger—that a certain germ has caused it, or that he can give it to another, or that another can "catch" it from him. But when the cells cannot get what they need, we say that the person has "caught" some kind of disease—some microbe has entered the laboratory of the human body. Does it seem reasonable?

What really occurs is this : The cells break down and disintegrate, because there is nothing, or not enough material given, to supply or replace the waste. As the functions are disturbed, this waste matter is not carried out of the body, but remains, clogging and poisoning the system. The little drain tiles which carry off the excess moisture and the poisons of the body are clogged and the surplus heat and moisture cannot escape; then fever, so called, results. If these little vents of the human body are not soon restored to their normal function, the patient dies. Give a stove too much fuel and close all the drafts, and the fire will go out. A person who eats more than the body requires, keeps the intestinal tract filled with fermenting food (just as a stove or furnace may be filled with clinkers), for there is not enough gastric juice to break it up and digest it. Auto-intoxication results and the intestinal tract is flooded with poison. Thus it is that such a person is always among the first to "catch" any so-called disease.

We give the engines that run our machinery a great deal more intelligent care than we give the dynamo that runs the physical machinery. A good machinist spends much time over his engine. He uses reason and common sense and knows that if his engine is clogged with oil or dirt it will not run easily and smoothly and he cannot expect to get maximum power from it. Why should physical machinery differ in this respect from artificial mechanism ? Instead of using reason and giving the physical furnace the right proportion and quantity of fuel—what do we do ? We eat, because it tastes good, a greater amount than we need, often suffering extreme discomfort.

When an article of food spoils, or a dead body starts to decompose, we do not say that a germ or microbe caused it— we know that it was because of atmospheric conditions; but we do realize that flies and maggots are formed from the decaying mass, and, if left alone, will consume it and die. The flies and maggots did not come until there was dead (so-called) matter present, for that is nature's method of removing it.

There are many kinds of material in the human body, and each is used for a definite purpose. For instance, there is much fibrin, which is a constituent of the tissue of the body. This needs the inorganic cell-salt, chloride of potassium (Kali Mur), to combine with it and make it functional. If the system is deficient in this cell-salt, the fibrin is not able to do its work becomes non-functional—and, if not carried off by any of the means which Mother Nature employs, it clogs the mechanism. Then we have a cough, or pneumonia sets in, or perchance we "catch" typhoid. The same thing causes it all, namely, a deficiency in chloride of potassium. Microbes are found—yes—but they are the product of decaying matter.

Away off in some secluded mountain home, one of the members of a family is taken with typhoid and dies. None of the others have it. If caused by a germ, what prevented the entire family from "catching" it?

An intelligent understanding of the composition and the functions of the body will enable any one to interpret the signals or calls sent out, and immediately supply the material that is lacking. One should understand that "All things work together for good," that the amount of food should be regulated, plenty of rest and the right amount of exercise be taken at the right time. Then a combination of the twelve cell-salts found in the body should be taken systematically in order to supply the deficiency in the human laboratory.

When the deficiency occurs, the patient, not being at ease, imagines that something must be the cause of the so-called pain, fever or unrest; and, in this, he is encouraged by the Doctor, who coins a Latin or Greek word to give standing and personality to the myth. The condition of not-at-ease arises because the blood, not being perfectly organized blood, does not properly feed and nourish the nerves, muscles and other tissues of the body, and, then, a call or dispatch is sent to the throne of understanding, asking that the lacking principle may be supplied.

These words, asking for the workmen to build new tissues into the human organism have, through the grossest ignorance, been given names in Latin or Greek, clothed with the tinsel of so-called scientific authority, and the people have been called upon to recognize and bow down in fear before the devils thus let loose.

An irreverent writer not long ago said that the romances of the present day were written by scientists, and that Rider Haggard, with "She" and "King Solomon's Mines," was but a dabster in comparison. A short time ago the Homeopathic Envoy said : "The march of science is preceded by an ever-increasing horde of Greek and Latin terms which stupefy the brain of the unscientific who seeks to comprehend them."

Among the latest of these words to carry dismay to the learned and unlearned is "phagocyte." Occasionally the editor of a daily paper is seen struggling with this foreigner, as though he knew all about him, and in late medical journals he may be seen stalking across the pages of some of the heavyweights. Of course, no one would display his ignorance by asking what sort of a thing a "phagocyte" is ; so we will look up his pedigree in the lexicons. The word "phagocyte" is derived from the Greek "Phagein", to eat, and "cytos", a hole or cavity, and really means an eater with capacity—a ravenous eater—but, according to the scientific gentleman, a "Phagocyte" is an eater of bacilli. Now, no doubt, the grand idea becomes apparent: turn the phagocytes loose in the system and let them run out the bacilli, as ferrets run rats out of a barn. One learned editor of a great daily, in the early days of lymph, suggested that it was a phagocyte, and discoursed most learnedly on the vast fields this new discovery of science opened up, and speculated as to whether each breed of bacilli had its own phagocyte or whether one breed of phagocyte could sail in and wipe up the floor with the most ferocious bacilli.

One question, however, has not yet been considered, and we respectfully suggest that science turn its light in that direction. After the pugnacious phagocyte has cleaned out the bacilli, what creature shall we turn loose in our insides to fight the phagocyte?

For the benefit of those who wish to know what the phagocyte may be called upon to contend with, I will mention some of the latest discoveries in the realm of the microbe : Man's liver may be infested with the terrible *distomum hepaticum*, while that of mutton suffers from *distomum lanceolatum*. The rabbit whisks about with coccidium oviform in his inwards, while man and cow both furnish habitation for the gentle *echinococcus polymorphus*. Man alone seems to have the distinction of entertaining the aristocratic *bothriocephalus latus* and that freebooter of the highway, *ankylostomum duo-denale*. The sporting couple, *dochimus tringoncephalus* and *stenocephalias*, seek the society of hunting dogs only ; first cousins to these, but rather more aristocratic, are the broth-ers, *sclerostoum hypostomum* and *tetracanthum*, who ride in horses ; while the diserputable family on whom all well-reg-ulated microbes look down, that is, the *strongylicontortus*, *fillicolus*, *strigocus* and *retortorformis*, dwell amid ships in goats and such like plebeans. But the most noted of all is the musical *dochmius atenocephalus*, the intimate of the cat, which, as further research will no doubt reveal, must be the microbe of all attempts to reach high C.

But Virchow's researches completely overthrow the germ or microbe theory and clearly prove that disease is caused by a lack of some constituent of the blood at the part affected and not by germs or bacilli.

The human system can use its constituent parts only; the cells are not fed—they feed themselves. They reject what they do not need. It cannot be forced upon them, except to the detriment or death of the body. Our vital forces are at once set to work to rid the system of anything and every-thing that does not belong to our organism and will not as-similate with blood, bone, muscle or other tissues.

Calomel, quinine, aconite, belladonna, salicylic acid, opium and the thousand and one poisons used in the "regular" medical practice are not constituent parts of the blood—are not found in the human organism, and, when taken into the system, set up their own action for the abnormal condition called disease and are worse than the disease itself.

Calomel does not cure; it simply sets up a diarrhoea in place of constipation. Opium does not cure; it simply causes paralysis of the nerve centers, in place of neuralgia. Those who take poisons and yet recover, do so in spite of both the disease and the drugs. The normal condition is restored through the natural processes. The so-called medicines have no part in the restoration. No improvement can be made on the human organism in this respect. The constituent part so four bodies, when perfectly balanced, keep all in harmony. When an abnormal condition arises, harmony can be restored by restoring the balance, but not by introducing a poison into the system. The disease may be changed to one that manifests itself in a different manner, but the patient is not cured. The word poison has but one definition, that is, an agent which, when taken into the stomach or blood, produces either disease or death. Therefore, by no possibility can poison cure.

When the microscope first revealed the fact that there is no inert matter—that all so-called matter is life in operation, even in the crystal and diamond—the scientists were frightened out of their wits. They saw God face to face, named Him "microbes" and tried to kill Him with carbolic acid.

But "He that sitteth in the heavens laughed and had them in derision." Carbolic acid is one expression of "Omnipresent Life"—microbes are another expression. Add the two and you still have the life.

The true thing alone is orthodox and no length of time can sanctify error. Not many years ago, the State Board of Health of Louisiana caused cannon to be fired in the streets of New Orleans, expecting the concussion to kill the germs of yellow fever. Later, the Seers of medicine declared that mosquitos were the sole cause of this disease.

It is claimed by the adherents of the germ theory that so-called malarial conditions are caused by germs.

Dry air cures ague. Cold weather cures ague. Sodium sulphate (natrum sulphuricum, or sulphate of sodium) in 3th X-one of the cell-salts of the blood—cures ague. So, then, these must all be Royal Germ Killers. No, they supply deficiencies.

Ague is caused by an excess of water in the blood and dry air (cold air is dry air), furnishes an extra amount of oxygen to the blood through the lungs, and eliminates the excess of hydrogenoid gases or water.

Sodium sulphate molecules eliminate an excess of water from the system. Each molecule has the chemical force to carry two molecules of water. *No one ever has ague whose blood is properly supplied with* SODIUM SULPHATE, NO MATTER HOW MANY GERMS OF MALARIA MAY ASSAIL HIM. The Homeopathic News published the following editorial on the germ theory in 1892:

"It is to be hoped that no intelligent homeopathic believes in a microbic origin of disease. It may be a matter of interest to the physician to study the bacteriological accompaniments of a given malady—if the malady has any; but the idea, that the fullest knowledge of the particular bacillus that may be found in the body of the subject of a given disease is of practical benefit to anybody, is a mistake.

"For whether we empirically administer drugs, hoping to cure disease, or prescribe experimentally for the destruction of a bacillus known to us microscopically, is all one. Give us a specific for cholera, and we care not whether our specific cures by destroying certain bacilli, or by producing blood changes, or in any other way. Where there is no guiding law for the cure of disease, it is all try, try, try, let the cause within the organism be animal, vegetable, or mineral, known or unknown.

"But we do not believe that, if bacilli peculiar to certain maladies have been found, they are the cause of the diseased state, that they accompany, any more than we believe that the leaves on a tree are the cause of the existence of the tree.

"When a theory of the causation of disease is backed by names universally admitted to be as great as those that endorse the germ theory, intelligent men are willing to investigate it. This we have done most thoroughly; and we believe that theory to be erroneous from top to bottom, and from first to last. We have never found a particle of evidence that bacilli have been discovered—in the sense pretended by their 'discoverers.' They have undoubtedly been 'faked' to a very great extent, beyond doubt intentionally on the part of the chief promulgators of the germ theory. The medical profession cannot be blamed, if its members very much doubt whether those gentlemen themselves believe in their own theory, or in their own 'discoveries.' We have learned to know, that disease is not an entity, but a condition produced by deficiencies, and that germs are a product of these conditions and do not cause the conditions."

The remark is frequently heard that the baby "nursed" its sore throat or bad cold from its mother. The statement is not only dogmatic and crude, but in the light of Biochemistry, is un-scientific.

The new pathology claims to be able to scientifically demonstrate the fact that so-called disease is simply a condition, and not an entity that may be transferred from one to another. Therefore, the expression, "Caught it from its mother", cannot be correct.

But then, the question arises, "How shall certain facts be explained"? No one will venture to deny, that nursing infants are very liable to suffer from the same symptoms that manifest themselves in their mothers; and, when we take issue with the race belief as to the modus operandi, by which the condition of the mother appears in the child, it is meet that we should offer our reasons and suggest the true cause of the phenomena.

In order to make the matter clear, I will offer an illustration Suppose a child, say five or six years of age, should be fed on a certain kind of grain, known to be deficient in phosphate of lime, and should, as a consequence, suffer from the disease or condition known as rickets, rachitis, admitted by all schools to be caused by a deficiency of the lime salts of the blood. In such case, no one would maintain that the grain gave the child the rickets, or that it caught it from the grain, but rather, that the grain, being deficient in lime, but not in albumen, furnished the blood with a sufficient quantity of organic matter, but not enough mineral or inorganic material to build up true bone structure.

Now for the application. Before the mother (or any one else) can have a cold or sore throat, there must be a deficiency in one or more of the inorganic cell-salts, or tissue builders, of the blood. Let us suppose the salt, that has fallen below the maximum, to be potassium chloride (kali mur), and, as a consequence, a certain portion of fibrin, not having workmen—molecules of kali mur,—to use, was thrown out by the circulation and clogged the parotid gland or tonsils, or other glands, or caused irritation to the membrane in nasal passages, or larynx, bronchial tubes, or pleura, or clogged the air cells of the lungs. In such case, is it not reasonable to suppose the mother's milk would be deficient in the cell-salt kali mur, and that the child, in accordance with the law laid down above, would also suffer from the result of the deficiency, as did the mother ?

As to germs, or bacilli, or microbes, etc., they swarm throughout all nature. They are Omnipresent Life in operation. They adhere to membranes in unhealthy conditions, but do not affect healthy ones.

Decaying organic matter produces microbes that exist while the process of decay goes on, feed upon it and disappear with it and return to the elements from which they were materialized.

DIPHTHERIA

Let me call your attention to the pathology of diphtheria (Greek for membrane), that scourge which baffles the skill of the regular practitioner, although his office walls are decorated with diplomas written in Latin. In venous blood fibrin amounts to three in one thousand parts; when the molecules of chloride of potassium fall below the standard in the blood, fibrin thickens, causing what is known as pleurisy, pneumonia, catarrh, diphtheria, etc. When the circulation fails to throw out the thickened fibrin via the glands or mucous membrane, it may stop the action of the heart. Embolus is a Latin word, meaning "little lump" or balls; therefore, to die of embolus, or "heart failure", generally means that the heart action was stopped by little lumps of fibrin clogging the auricles and ventricles of the heart.

In diphtheria we have a striking illustration of the effect of deficiencies. Electric changes and disturbances in the atmosphere cause a deficiency in molecules of potassium chloride.

But some one may ask how atmospheric or electric states and changes affect our cell structure, so that conditions called disease appear. It is well known that there are subtle influences which, although invisible, produce well-defined results. The barometer rises or falls while the degree of heat or cold remains unchanged. Every baker knows there are influences unseen and unfelt by him that prevent his yeast from rising. They are simply antagonistic influences.

When these influences are adverse to man, he suffers just in proportion to his inability to meet the opposing forces. The forces that injure him first act through the pneumogastric nerve, disturb the gastric juice and break up the chain of molecules of iron. This diminishes the outer circulation, the feet and hands are probably chilled, the pores of the skin close and the waste matter, the dead cells that should be cast off through these avenues, are turned upon the inner organs. It is the law of conservation of energy that motion is changed to heat ; and when the machinery of our being is set more actively to work to rid the system of this waste matter, the increased circulation which follows produces an excess of heat which is called fever.

In diphtheria, which, as said before, is caused by a deficiency in molecules of potassium chloride, these salts with fibrin and albuminous substances find their way to the tonsils and thymus gland and form a plastic exudation. From the supply constantly thrown out of circulation the accumulation keeps grow- ing until the patient dies of suffocation. There is no specific diphtheria germ.

CHOLERA

Cholera is a Greek term, derived from "chole," meaning bile. Cholera is a chemical condition characterized by violent emesis, diarrhoea, abdominal pains and cramps. The alvine discharge, resembling rice water, with floculent sediment, indicates great disturbance in the gray matter of the brain and a breaking up of the nerve fluids; also a non-functional operation of water, which shows that sodium chloride molecules have fallen below the standard of balance, and, therefore, fail to properly control and distribute water. The chief cause of the acute attack is the breaking away of water from blood and serum.

But the primary cause is an over-supply of water in the blood, caused by an atmosphere heavily laden with moisture. Cholera does not thrive in temperature below 70 degrees, although cases sometimes appear after the temperature has fallen below 70 degrees, but the blood has become over-loaded with water during the time the heat was great enough to cause excessive humidity. Persons who have not been exposed to humid air, do not yield to the disease, although they may come in contact with a cholera patient. Therefore, my contention is, that an excess of moisture (pure water, H_2O), is the cause of cholera, and that germs, microbes, bacilli, etc., are concomitants of the chemical break in the blood and nerve fluids. Pure water may thin the fluids of the liver until fatal results are produced.

The so-called cholera bacillus lives on the heteroplasm caused by the molecular break in the chain of the mineral salts in the blood. Sodium sulphate regulates the amount of water in the blood by its chemical power to eliminate the surplus water. But when the air is overcharged with aqueous vapor, sodium sulphate molecules often become overworked in their efforts to eliminate water, and a deficiency arises, leaving the "water logged" system in the condition known as cholera, yellow fever, or malaria (bad air), according to the degree of the deficiency coupled with planetary aspects at the particular time. In most instances the person with too much water in the blood will simply suffer from the condition known as chills and fever, or malaria. The chill is a spasm of the muscular nervous and vascular system, making a supreme effort to wring out and throw off the surplus water in the blood that would have been done by the catalyic action of sodium sulphate, had there been a reinforcement of that cell-salt to equal the amount of water taken into the arteries through the lungs by breathing air over- charged with humid vapor.

The heat (called fever), that follows a chill, is but the result of rapid circulation (friction), caused by nature's efforts to carry oxygen to all tissues of the body to supply the deficiency caused by the spasm or chill.

If the amount of water in the blood should be excessive, and planetary angles favorable, the fluids of the liver and pancreas break away. The liver first empties its contents, and the discharge is colored with bile, but, later on, the fluids are clear, or like rice water, which indicates water and nerve fluids. All other outlets of the body seem closed except the intestinal tract. The pores close and the urinary secretions become dried at their source.

In 1852 Peyton wrote, in a treatise on cholera : "Very remarkable results have been found to follow the injection into the veins of a dilute solution of saline matter resembling, as nearly as possible, the inorganic salts which have been drained away."

During a cholera epidemic in 1877 the famous Dr. Koch went to India to search for the cause of that dread disease. A microscopic examination of the cistern water (it had never been examined before) revealed bacilli, (Latin for little sticks), and Dr. K. sagely concluded that he had found the cause of cholera. The discovery was telegraphed to "earth's remotest bounds", and the fatted calf was killed and eaten, while the medical world held "high jinks"; but they could not find anything that would kill the germs without being quite as fatal to the patient as cholera. After colder weather came and the cholera epidemic subsided, some doctors who were skeptical about the microbe nonsense (quacks, I suppose), went to India to search for the dead germs, thinking, of course, that as there were no more cholera, there could be no more germs; but, on examining the cistern water, they found the bacilli lively and in good health, but they refused to bite anymore. It seems that these microbes only got real hungry during the hot weather.

PNEUMONIA

The following, on pneumonia, was taken from the Biochemic System of Medicine, published in 1894 : "No abnormal condition with which suffering mortals are afflicted has such terrors for the average physician as pneumonia, unless it be typhoid or typhus fever. The New York Medical Record, of late date, contained the following: 'Pneumonia is attended at the present day with an ever-increasing mortality—so high, in fact, as to constitute a reproach to medical science.'

"A prominent physician of Philadelphia wrote as follows 'The mortality of pneumonia in Philadelphia has increased, and is greater today than it was thirty years ago.'

" 'The errors of thirty years ago have been intensified. Still larger doses of nauseating drugs have been administered, and the local treatment has increased in severity.' The microbe theory, the fallacy of the age, has piled error on error, until the wonder is that any one recovers from pneumonia under the treatment. The trouble all along has been the failure of the medical profession to understand just what causes the condition of : 'not at ease,' in pneumonia.

The medical text-books and dictionaries will tell you "That pneumonia, or lung fever, is inflammation of one or more lobes of the lungs;'" but make no attempt to explain what inflammation really is or what produces it. These books tell us that certain anatomical changes take place; that firm or solid exudation is found in pulmonary alveoli, but do not tell of what the exudation is composed or how it reached the air cells. We are graciously informed that 'there is intense congestive hyperaemia' ; that 'there is red hepatization, in which the lung is bulky, heavy and airless, its red tint due to extravastated corpuscles and distended capillaries or gray hepatization, due to decolorization of the exudation and pulmonary anaemia or colliquation and resolution.'

"The above may be very learned, but the student cannot help but wonder what the cause of it all is, and what on earth he will do to prevent it.

"Biochemistry alone explains the cause of the abnormal condition called pneumonia and offers the cure.

"Atmospheric electrical changes so operate on the human system as to cause a deficiency in iron and other inorganic mineral salts of the blood, which lowers the vitality and causes the pores to close. The waste matter, the exudation from the skin, is then turned inward and seeks an outlet. The fluids of the body, water, albumen, etc., serve as carriers for the effete matter.

"Of course the circulation is increased, for two reasons: (a) To carry off the decaying organic matter; (b) Because of a deficiency in iron the blood is poorly supplied with oxygen, which, as is well known, has an affinity for iron ; and the rapid motion is nature's effort to make the limited iron supply do the work of the maximum amount.

"If, in getting rid of the waste, nature directs it to the lungs, and this causes injury to lung structure, as the decaying, vitiated, organic matter surely will, if in sufficient quantity, the medical profession have been pleased to name it pneumonia. Catarrh, bronchitis, etc., have the same pathology.

The decaying organic matter, the heteroplasm, deposited in connective tissue and membranes during the inflammatory stage, of course, must be gotten rid of, but the circulation will attend to it, if the tools are furnished to work with. While this work is being carried on, there will be disturbances, coughs, etc., but the only rational way to do is to supply the blood with the vital principles needed, so the work may be done."

The pathology of all venereal diseases is the same as the pathology of any disease. See special article on Syphilis in the "Biochemic System of Medicine", page 353.

LESSON I.

The chemical formula and Physiological action of the Cell Salts of the human Organism.

As bone is the foundation of the animal structure, I will commence with the bone builder.

Phosphate of Lime—Synonyms: Calcarea Phosphoricum, Calcium Phosphate. Formula $Ca_3(PO_4)_2$.

Phosphoric acid, dropped in lime water, precipitates this salt in crude form. Let the student bear in mind that this lime-salt, as well as all the others, must be triturated with sugar of milk up to at least the third decimal, or potency, in order that the molecules may become separated from the mass to the extent that they can be taken up by the delicate mucous membrane absorbents of the stomach and intestinal tract and thus enter the blood vessels.

As to the best decimal potency to give, to supply deficiencies in the mineral salts, there is quite a difference in opinion. Many of the homeopathic physicians contend for higher potencies, from sixth up to two hundredths, while bio-chemists generally use the third and sixth.

Bone tissue consists of about 57 per cent lime phosphate. The lime salt has chemical affinity for albumen. While there is a certain degree of affinity between each of the cell-salts and albumen—albumen being the base of all organic mat-ter—the operation of calcarea phosphate with albumen is greatest. The salt chemically unites with albumen, carries it and uses it as cement to build bone tissues. Bone also con-tains carbonate of soda, magnesium phosphate and sodium chloride, but lime phosphate is the chief builder of bone tissue, and it follows, as a logical sequence, that it is the principal salt deficient in all so-called diseases of bone struc-ture.

The gelatine found in bone tissue is formed by the union of albumen, oil, carbon, lime and phosphate in certain proportion. Of course, there is a small amount of other principles in bone, such as magnesia, sodium chloride, silicia, etc. When the molecules of lime phosphate fall below the normal in amount and thus fail to keep up the supply of bone material, some symptoms of bone disease manifest. Again, a lack in the proper amount of this builder, in some instances, causes an anemic condition, for bone material (lime and albumen) is the foundation of bodily structure.

Under certain conditions, dependent on deficiencies in other cell-salts, a break in the molecular chain of lime phosphate will cause an outflow of albumen through the kidneys. Why should the escape of albumen via the kidneys be named Bright's Disease ? It seems that the fact of the loss of albumen in this manner was first discovered in the case of a hospital patient named Bright, and although many Browns, Joneses and Smiths die in a regular and orthodox manner from the same cause that cut off the immortal Bright, the medical profession still dignify the disease by the original label.

The very same albumen that causes "Bright's Disease," if thrown out through the nasal passage, is called catarrh (from the Greek: To drop down).

If the albumen reaches the skin, by disintegration, or fermentation, it causes pimples, eruptions, eczema, etc. If any one derives pleasure from these names, well and good, let them use them, but chemistry knows nothing whatever about them.

A great deficiency in lime phosphate may cause albumen to accumulate in some gland and there disintegrate and flow out in pus, or heteroplasm, which is called scrofula by the old school physicians. Scrofula is derived from scrofula, Latin for sow. Maybe the ancients believed the pork eaters were more liable to the disease than were the Jews.

The lime molecules are found in the fluids of digestion and assimilation, and when there is a lack of the proper amount of these workers, the digestive juices become negative, lose their proper rate of motion, or catalyc action, ferment and thus produce gas, acid condition, etc. When lime phosphate and sodium phosphate, the alkaline salts, are deficient, acids, together with albuminous substance, may settle in the joints and thus render synovial fluids non-functional; thereby, causing pain, stiffness and swelling of the joints. Just why this chemical fact must needs have the word rheumatism tacked to it does not appear. The word rheumatism is derived from rheum—to flow out.

Biochemistry does not deal with names and effects; it deals with causes, the chemistry of life and the law of supplying deficiencies.

Medical writers of late have adopted the term albuminuria in place of Bright's Disease, which very well describes the symptom or effect, but does not hint at the cause of the symptom.

Biochemistry seeks to learn the particular food called for by pains, exudations, swelling, inflammations, etc. Nature never calls for anything that is not a constituent part of the organism demanding supply.

Blood is the base of the physical life of man, and as a man's blood is, so is his health.

A word about potencies: We are told by the analytical chemists, that a quart of milk contains only the six-millionth part of a grain of iron. An infant fed on milk receives one milligram of iron in a half pint of milk, which is only the fourth part of the above minute fraction of one part of a grain of iron. It would seem from the above that four milligrams of iron daily is sufficient to feed all the cells that are known to contain and consequently require iron. This being the case, it surely can require but an infinitesimal amount of iron to supply the links in a broken molecular chain.

With these demonstrated facts before us, high potencies are no longer vague theories and the butt of jokes. On the contrary, they are man's best endeavor to imitate Nature's processes.

LESSON II.

Sulphate of Lime—Synonyms: Calcium Sulphate, Calcarea Sulphate, Calci Sulphos, Gypsum, Plaster of Paris.

Formula—$CaSo_4$.

This salt can be obtained by precipitating a solution of calcium chloride of lime with dilute sulphuric acid.

Sulphate of lime should never be used below the 6th decimal trituration.

Tissue is composed of living cells. By giving a tissue builder the deficient mineral salt in such a dose, fineness and amount as can be assimilated by the growing cells, the most wonderful and speedy restoration to healthy functions is brought about in every case of curable disease. We know that these minerals are infinitesimally subdivided in the different kinds of food we take, thus rendering them capable of being assimilated by the cells. The cells of each tissue-group receive their own special and peculiar cell-salt.

The sulphate of lime is the chief builder of epithelial tissue, or to be more exact, the chief sustainer for the chloride of potassium, as will be shown in Lesson V, is the worker in fibrine and has much to do in the formation of epithelium.

Lime sulphate furnishes the cohesive, or plaster, substance to sustain the integrity of tissue. The chief symptom of disease, indicating a deficiency in the lime salt, is suppuration or the discharge of pus, which is an exudation formed by the breaking down, disintegration and fermentation of epithelial cells. Lime phosphate, by its union with albuminoids, assists chloride of potassium to form epithelial tissue, or, at least, to hold it intact by its cohesive quality.

The third stage of catarrh, bronchitis, lung disease, boils, carbuncles, ulcers, abscesses or exudations from any part of the body, indicates a lack of this tissue-builder. Lime sulphate, not only sustains epithelial tissue, but, when administered in case of suppuration, it cleans out the heteroplasm from the interstices of tissue by causing the infiltrated parts to discharge their contents readily, which prevents slow decay and injury to surrounding healthy cells.

The action of lime sulphate is opposite to the work of silica (see Lesson XII), which hastens the process of suppuration in a natural manner, while the lime closes up a process that has continued too long. Thus are we made to realize the marvelous intelligence manifested in life's procession in the organism of man.

Chemical affinity is but a synonym of infinite intelligence in operation in the functions of man.

LESSON III.

Fluoride of Lime—Synonyms: Calcaria Flurica, Calcium Fluoride.

Chemical Formula—$Ca F_2$.

This salt is formed by the union of lime and fluorine.

The inorganic salts are the workers, controlled and directed by Infinite Intelligence, which perform the ceaseless miracle of creation or formation.

It is quite as important for a student of Biochemistry to understand the process by which certain cell-salts operate to supply a deficiency as it is to know for what a particular symptom calls.

Elastic fibre, the chief organic substance in rubber, is formed by a chemical union of the fluoride of lime with albumen, oil, etc. Therefore, we find this salt dominant in the elastic fibre of the body, in the enamel of teeth and connective tissue.

A lack of this salt in proper amount causes a relaxed condition of muscular tissue, falling of the womb and varicose veins. Sometimes there is a non-functional combination of this salt with oil and albumen which forms a solid deposit, causing swellings of stony hardness; it is a sort of incomplete fibre with other lime salts and vitiated fluids of the body.

There is one particular symptom that is worthy of note in connection with the pathology of this salt. When a deficiency exists in these makers of elastic fibre in the connective tissue between cerebellum and cerebrum, the lower and upper brain, it causes groundless fears of financial ruin. It seems that the relaxed condition of connective tissue, causing a sagging of the structure of cerebellum, thereby breaks the flow of the electric or magnetic currents from the cerebrum.

The student will now see that it is exceedingly easy to diagnose disease from the viewpoint of Biochemic Pathology. No guesswork here. Go to twenty or one hundred Biochemic physicians and give the same symptoms to each, and you will get the same prescriptions in every case.

It does not matter under what name of disease a disturbance in elastic fibre appears, a study of the chemistry of life has made clear the fact that a break in the molecular chain of lime fluoride salt is always the cause of the phenomenon.

The proportion of fluorine in the human organism is less than that of iron. From analytical facts it is found that fluorine in milk is only present in decimilligrams, and yet we are confronted by the fact that this infinitesimal amount is sufficient to sustain all the elastic fibre of muscular tissue, enamel of teeth and connective tissue.

Professor Leibig, in his chemical letters, accentuates the importance of high potencies or dilutions, as follows:

"At the temperature of the hydrochloric acid, diluted with one-thousandth part of water, readily dissolves the fibrine of meat and the gluten of cereals, and this solvent power is decreased, not increased, when the acid solution is made stronger."

Why should we search Latin and Greek lexicons to find a name for the result of a deficiency in some of the mineral constituents of blood. If we find a briar in our flesh, we say so in the plainest speech; we do not say,"I have got the briatitis or sprintralgia."

When we know that a deficiency in the cell-salts of the blood causes the symptoms which medical ignorance dignified and personified with names of which nobody knows the meaning, we will know how to scientifically heal by the unalterable law of the chemistry of life. When we learn the cause of disease, then and not before, will we prevent disease.

Professor Valentin, the well known physiologist, says: "Nature works everywhere with an infinite number of small magnitudes, which can be preceived by our relatively obtuse organs of sense only when in masses. The smallest picture which our eyes preceive proceeds from millions of waves of light. A granule of salt that we are hardly able to taste contains myriads of groups of atoms which no sentient eye will ever view."

LESSON IV.

Phosphate of Iron.
Synonyms—Ferrum phosphate, Ferri Phosphas.
Formula—$Fe_3 (P O_4)^2$.

Phosphate of iron may be prepared by mixing sodium phosphate with sulphate of iron. The salt precipitated by this union is filtered, washed, dried and rubbed to a powder.

The iron phosphate should not be used below the sixth (decimal trituration), as large doses of iron, as in tinctures, have a bad effect on the mucous lining of the stomach, injure the teeth and utterly fail to supply iron to the blood where it is needed to carry oxygen, the life giver.

One red blood corpuscle does not exceed the one hundred and twenty millionth of a cubic inch. There are more than three million such cells in one drop of blood, and these cells carry the iron in the blood. How necessary, then, to administer the salts of iron to hungry cells in the most minute molecular form.

Each one of the twelve inorganic salts has its own sphere of function and curative action. Thus we find the phosphate of iron molecularly deficient in all fevers and inflammatory symptoms.

Health depends on a proper amount of iron phosphate in the blood, for the molecules of this salt have chemical affinity for oxygen and carry it to all parts of the organism. When these oxygen carriers are deficient, the circulation is increased in order to conduct a sufficient amount of oxygen to the extremities with the diminished quantity of iron, exactly as seven men must move faster to do the work often. This increased rate of motion of the blood is changed to heat, caused by friction, otherwise known as the "conservation of energy."

This heat, or increase in the temperature of blood, has been named fever, from the Latin word fevre, meaning "To boil out."

The writer fails to see any relevancy between the word fever and a deficiency in iron phosphate molecules in the blood. From Hippocrates to Koch you will not find a true definition of fever outside of the Biochemic theory.

It is not simply the heat that causes distress in a fever patient, but it is the lack of oxygen in the blood due to a deficiency in iron, the carrier of oxygen.

A molecular break in the links of the chain of iron disturbs the continuity of other salts and thus causes more deficiencies. The chloride of potassium (see Lesson V), is usually the first salt called for after the disturbance in iron.

These mighty workers, iron and oxygen, cause all the blood in the body to pass through the heart every three minutes. The lungs contain about one gallon of air at their usual degree of inflation. We breathe, on an average, 1200 breaths per hour; inhale 600 gallons of air per hour and 24,000 gallons daily; and iron and oxygen are the wizards that perform the miracle. When a deficiency in iron occurs, nature— chemical affinity draws the blood inward from the surface of the body, in order to conserve this life force so that the vital organs, heart, stomach, liver, lungs and brain, may continue to function. But the poor surface circulation allows the pores to close, and thus the waste matter that should escape by this route is turned upon the inner organs, causing exudations, catarrh, pneumonia, pleurisy, etc. But these names are of no consequence. The student will clearly see that iron phosphate is indicated by certain symptoms in whatever part of the organism they may appear. Iron molecules give toughness and strength to the walls of veins and arteries and the minute blood vessels called capillaries (hair-like) and are, therefore, the remedy for hemorrhages.

A child may touch a button that will start a complex machine operating, and yet not understand the science of physics or the mechanism of the machine. So many systems of healing may be the means of starting into action the workmen that may have become dormant. But when the workmen are deficient in the organism, man's body is a chemical formula in operation, it would seem to be the sensible thing to do to furnish the needed chemicals.

There is but one law of chemical operation in vegetable or animal life. When a man understands and co-operates with that operation, he will call into being whatsoever he will; his organism will show forth the glory of omnipresent spirit and its "fearful and wonderful" mechanism will be the crowning glory of earth.

LESSON V.

The Chloride of Potash, or Potassium.

Synonyms—Potassium chloride, Kali Muriaticum, Kali Chloratum, Kali Chloridum, Potassi Chloridum.

Formula—K Cl.

This salt must not be confused with the chlorate of potash, a poison, chemical formula $K.CLO_3$.

Chloride of potash may be obtained by neutralizing pure aqueous hydrochloric acid with pure potassium carbonate or hydrate.

The cell-salt kali-muriaticum (Potassium chloride) is the mineral worker of the blood that forms fibrin and properly diffuses it through the tissues of the body.

Kali mur molecules are the principal agents used in the chemistry of life to build fibrin into the human organism. The skin that covers the face contains the lines and angles that give expression and thus differentiate one person from another.

In venous blood fibrin amounts to three in one thousand parts; when the molecules of Kali mur fall below the standard in the blood, fibrin thickens, causing what is known as pleurisy, pneumonia, catarrh, diphtheria, etc. When the circulation fails to throw out the thickened fibrin via the glands or mucous membrane, it may stop the action of the heart. Embolus is a Latin word, meaning little lump, or balls ; therefore, to die of embolus, or "heart failure" generally means that the heart's action was stopped by little lumps of fibrin clogging the auricles and ventricles of the heart.

When the blood contains the proper amount of kali mur, fibrin is functional and the symptoms referred to above do not manifest.

Biochemistry has discovered the fact that the cause of embolus, diphtheria, fibroid tumors and fibrinus exudations are not the result of an over-supply of fibrin itself. These symptoms are due to a deficiency in the potash molecules that work with fibrin, diffuse it throughout the organism and build it into tissue.

LESSON VI.

The Phosphate of Potash.

Synonyms—Potassium Phosphate, Kali Phosphoricum, Potassii Phosphas.

Formula— $K_3 PO_4$.

It may be prepared by mixing aqueous phosphoric acid with a sufficient quantity of potash, hydrate or carbonate, until the reaction is slightly alkaline and evaporating. Triturate to 3d or 6th X.

This salt is the great builder of the postive brain cells. Kali phos. unites with albumen and by some subtle alchemy trans- mutes it and forms gray brain matter.

When the chemical possibilities of this brain builder are fully understood, insane asylums will go out of fashion.

Nervous disorders of all kinds, sleeplessness, paresis, paralysis, irritability, despondency, pessimism, making mountains out of mole hills, crossing broken bridges that do not exist, and borrowing trouble and paying compound interest on the note—all these and many more abnormal conditions that make life a burden are caused by a break in the molecular chain of this nerve and brain builder.

Man has been deficient in understanding because his brain receiver did not vibrate to certain subtle influences; the dynamic cells in gray matter of nerves were not finely attuned and did not respond—hence, sin, or falling short of understanding.

From the teachings of the Chemistry of Life we find that the basis of brain or nerve fluid is a certain mineral salt known as potassium phosphate, or Kali Phos. Kali phosphate is the greatest healing agent known to man, because it is the chemical base of material expression and understanding.

Anything that prevents the formation of new cells as fast as old cells decay or die disturbs the equilibrium and some pain or other symptom indicates that all is not right. This phenomenon is simply a telegraphic dispatch sent along the nerves to the brain to inform the Ego, the Throne of Understanding, that a deficiency exists—that the material necessary to keep up the processes of life is not sufficiently supplied at a certain place.

And why is it not supplied? Health is that condition of the system where a certain proper degree of heat is maintained, where there is a proper blending of positive and negative electrical influences, and, where every tissue of the body is properly supplied with the right amount of blood, containing all of the elements requisite for building the new cells. This condition can be secured or maintained only by a proper amount of suitable physical exercise, a proper amount of food of a right kind, taken at reasonable intervals, and a judicious adaptation of the clothing to the temperature and occupation.

Anything which breaks up this balance injures, just according to the degree of the adverse influence. If over-eating, the alimentary canal becomes clogged with undigested food, the nutrition, which should be set free to transude through the walls of the intestines to be taken up by the absorbents and carried into the circulation, remains in the fibre of the food and passes out of the body, and, of course, a deficiency at once exists in the blood.

Any disturbance in the molecular motion of these cell-salts in living tissues constitutes disease. This disturbance canbe rectified, and the equilibrium re-established by administering a small dose of the same mineral salts in molecular form. The Biochemic System of Medicine is founded on physiology, anatomy, cellular pathology and chemistry, as set forth by Schuessler, Huxley, Tyndall, Virchow, Liebig, Valentin, Goullon, Moleschott and Walker, of Europe, and many noted scientists of our own land. Professor Moleschott, of the University of Rome, says in his work, The Circulation of Life: "The structure and vital power of the organs are conditional upon the necessary quantity of the inorganic salts of the blood."

Dr. Schuessler says that these words awakened in him the idea of employing for healing purposes the inorganic salts alone. Schuessler says in his Therapeutics : "My system or method of procedure is direct Biochemistry, because I use only tissue cell-salts, substances which are homogeneous to those contained in the diseased tissue. These salts, used properly, in a proper potency, cure all curable disease."

LESSON VII.

Sulphate of Potash.

Synonyms—Potassium Sulphate, Kali Sulphos, Potassae Sulphos, Kali Sulphate.

Formula— K_2SO_4.

The microscope reveals the fact that, when the body is in health, little jets of steam are constantly escaping from the seven million pores of the skin. The human body is a furnace and steam engine. The stomach and bowels burn food by chemical operation as truly as the furnace of a locomotive consumes by combustion. In the case of the locomotive the burning of coal furnishes force which vibrates water and causes an expansion (rate of motion) that we name steam.

The average area of skin is estimated to be about 2000 square inches. The atmospheric pressure, being fourteen pounds to the square inch, a person of medium size is subject to a pressure of 40,000 pounds.

Each square inch of skin contains 3500 sweat tubes, or perspiratory pores (each of which may be likened to a little drain tile) one-fourth of an inch in length, making an aggregate length of the entire surface of the body of 201,166 feet, or a title for draining the body nearly forty miles in length.

Let me repeat, for it is very important, the stomach is the furnace of man's body, and, by the process of digestion, burns up food and furnishes force to run the human engine, and thus enable it to inhale air, the material for blood, as water is the material for steam. In the manufacture of blood, through the complex operation of air passing through lung-cells, arteries, etc., a certain amount of water is changed to steam, a portion of which must escape through the safety valves provided by Divine Intelligence for that purpose. Sometimes the pores become clogged, and prevent the steam from escaping; then the vibration of the body changes and the person is sick. In many cases a disturbance in oil is the cause of the trouble. Potassium sulphate has an affinity for oil ; it is the maker and distributor of oil. When this salt falls below the standard in quantity, in the human organism, oil becomes non-functional—too thick, and thus clogs the pores.

And does it not seem strange that medical science, that boasts of such great progress, can invent no better term than "bad color" for these chemical results ?

Kali Sulph. is found in considerable quantities in scalp and hair. When this salt falls below the standard, dandruff or eruptions, secreting yellowish, thin, oily matter of falling out of hair, is the result.

Kali Sulph. is a wonderful salt, and its operation in the divine laboratory of man's body, where it manufactures oil, is the miracle of the chemistry of life.

Oil is made by the union of the sulphate of potassium (Potash) with albuminoids and aerial elements.

A deficiency of sulphate of potash in the molecules is the cause of oily, slimy, yellowish exudations from any orifice of the body, or from any glandular swellings, abscesses, cancers, etc.

LESSON VIII.

Phosphate of Magnesia.

Synonyms—Magnesium Phosphorica.

Formula—$Mg_3 PO_{4\,2}$

This cell-salt may be made by mixing Phosphate of Soda with Sulphate of Magnesia. This salt is found chiefly in the white fibres of nerves and muscles. The tissues of nerves and muscles are composed of many very fine threads or strands of different colors, each acting as a special telegraph wire, each one having a certain conductile power or quality, i. e., special chemical affinity—for certain organic substances, oil or albumen, through and by which the organism is materialized and the process or operations of life are carried on. The imagination might easily conceive the idea that these delicate infinitesimal fibres are strings of the Human Harp, and that molecular minerals are the fingers of infinite Energy, striking notes of some Divine Anthem.

The white fibres of nerves and muscles need the dynamic action of Magnesia Phosphate, especially to keep them in proper tune, or function, for, by its chemical action on albumen, the special fluid for white nerve or muscle fibre is formed. When the supply of this salt falls below the standard, cramps, sharp shooting pains, or some spasmodic condition, prevails. Such symptoms are simply calls of nature for more magnesia.

The human body is composed of perfect principles, gases, minerals, molecules or atoms; but these builders of flesh and bone are not always properly adjusted.

The planks or bricks used in building houses may be endlessly diversified in arrangement and yet be perfect material. Therefore, we must conclude that symptoms of disease are dispatches sent to the brain—the throne of understanding—calling for the worker, the builder, needed to carry on Life's work in flesh. Cases of Chorea (St. Vitus' dance) are cured by the proper use of magnesia phosphate. This salt is the great remedy for nearly all heart troubles, except embolus. (See Kali Mur., Lesson V.)

The white fibres in the delicate strands that compose the tissue of nerves are controlled by the molecules of magnesia; when these workers are deficient in amount, these live wires contract or cramp up in knots, of course, infinitely small, the effect of which is a sharp shooting pain, as in so-called neuralgia, or sciatica. The word neuralgia is from (a) Latin for nerves (b) Greek for pain, and therefore simply means nerve pain. English expresses the effect quite as well as other languages. But the idea generally prevails that neuralgia means a thing unknown and undefinable that causes the pain, and that the name of this unknown thing is neuralgia.

The pain is simply a dispatch, or words, asking for magnesia phosphate.

A deficiency of this salt in the muscular and nerve tissue of the walls of the stomach causes contraction, cramps, which reduces the cavity of the stomach. In order to meet this condition and prevent a collapse, such as is formed by natural chemical process from material at hand and by expansion, magnesium phosphate produces a counter-force that wards off more serious results. Magnesium phosphate relieves such conditions immediately, thus demonstrating the theory that to supply the deficient tissue-builder is the natural method of cure. The phosphate of lime of ten supplements magnesia. This wonderful salt is the true antispasmodic remedy. It has cured cases of chorea, or St. Vitus' dance, in from two to four weeks. For all heart troubles caused by distension of the cardiac portion of the stomach, thus interfering with the action of the heart, it is the sovereign remedy.

Dr. Baericke, one of the leading homeopathic physicians of the Pacific Coast, says : "Magnesia phosphate is a magnificent remedy in all spasmodic diseases."

It is plainly evident that the wonderful fluids of the human body are manufactured in the chemical laboratory of the organism. The particles of magnesia evidently contain within themselves the power and potency to create the white fibre nerve fluid by using albuminous substances as a basis, and then calling to its aid the spirit of life, oxygen. Each one of the inorganic salts knows how to make some fluid or tissue of the human machine. "And the tree bore twelve manner of fruits and its leaves were for the healing of the nations."

Like the phosphate of potash (see Lesson VI), magnesia phosphate is a nerve and brain salt, and, when we consider the wonders of the brain and its marvelous mechanism, we must recognize the great importance of the wizard workmen which labor for three score and ten years without an instant rest.

LESSON IX.

Sodium Chloride.

Synonyms—Natrum muriaticum, Sodii Chloridium, Chloruretum of Sodicum, Common table salt.

Formula—Na Cl.

A combination of sodium and chlorine forms the mineral known as common salt. This mineral absorbs water. The circulation or distribution of water in the human organism is due to the chemical action of the molecules of sodium chloride.

This inorganic cell-salt is the bearer and distributer of water. Sodium chloride must be triturated up to the 3d or 6th biochemic potency before using as an agent to supply deficiencies in the water carrier molecules arising from a lack of this salt.

Water constitutes over 70 per cent of the human body, therefore, the carriers of water must be in like proportion. There is more sodium chloride in the ashes of a cremated body than any of the 12 mineral salts, except the phosphate of lime, which composes 57 per cent of bone structure.

Through its affinity for water, this salt assists in carrying on the process of life in the human organism as well as in all vegetable tissue.

When there is a deficiency in the molecules of the water bearer, salt, the molecular continuity of water is broken, and, as a result, too much water will appear at a certain point and corresponding dryness or lack of water at other places. Example: Watery discharge from nasal passages and constipation of the bowels.

Sunstroke and delirium tremens are caused by a break in the supply of this salt, which causes water to press or crowd the membranes of the cerebellum (lower brain), and thus prevent the magnetic vibrations from the cerebrum (upper brain) from passing to the solar plexus, or central brain.

Crude soda cannot be taken up by mucous membrane absorb- ents and carried into the circulation. The sodium molecules found in the blood have been received from vegetable tissue which drew these salts from the soil in high potency. The mineral, or cell-salts, can also be prepared and are prepared in biochemic or homeopathic potency as the trituration of Nature's laboratory in the physiology of plant growth, and then, thoroughly mixed with sugar of milk and pressed into tablets ready to be taken internally, supply deficiencies in the human organism. A lack of the proper amount of these basic mineral salts, twelve in number, is the cause of all so-called disease.

Common table salt does not enter the blood, being too coarse to enter the delicate tubes of mucous membrane absorbent, but this salt does distribute water along the intestinal tract.

Professor Leibig says in his Chemical Letters, that muriatic acid, when diluted a thousand fold with water, dissolves, with ease, at the temperature of the body, fibrin and gluten, and this solvent power does not increase, but diminishes, if the proportion of acid in the dilution be increased.

Air contains 78 per cent of nitrogen gas, believed by scientists to be mineral in ultimate potency. Minerals are formed by the precipitation of nitrogen gas. Differentation is attained by the proportion of oxygen and aqueous vapor (hydrogen) that unites with nitrogen.

A deficiency in sodium chloride causes the water in the blood serum to become inert and non-functional. By its affinity for water, sodium chloride assists in the biological operation in blood and tissue.

As will be seen in Lesson XI, sodium sulphate eliminates an excess of water in the blood and thus regulates the supply; while sodium chloride properly distributes water in the physiology of animal or vegetable forms.

LESSON X.

Phosphate of Soda.

Synonyms—Natrum phosphate, Sodium phosphate, Natri Phosphate, Phosphos Natricus, Sodae Phosphate.

Formula—Na_2HPO_4 ; $_{12}H_2$; $Na_3 PO_4X_{12}H_2O$.

This alkaline cell-salt is made from bone ash or by neutralizing orthophosphoric acid with carbonate of sodium.

Sodium, or natrum, phosphate holds the balance between acids and normal fluids of the human body.

Acid is organic and can be chemically split into two or more elements, thus destroying the formula that makes the chemical rate of motion called acid.

Acid conditions are not due to an excess of acid in the blood, bile or gastric fluids. Supply the alkaline salt sodium phosphate, and acid will chemically change to normal fluids.

A certain amount of acid is necessary, and always present in the blood, nerve, stomach and liver fluids. The apparent excess of acid is nearly always due to a deficiency in the alkaline, salt.

Acid, in alchemical lore, is represented as Satan, Saturn, while sodium phosphate symbolizes Christ,Venus. An absence of the Christ principle gives license to Satan to run riot in the Holy Temple. The Advent of Christ drives the exile out with a whip of thongs. Reference to the temple, in the figurative language of the Bible and New Testament, always symbolizes the human organism. "Know ye not that your bodies are the Temple of the living God?"

Solomon's temple is an allegory of the physical body of man and woman. Soul—of man's temple—the house, church, Beth or temple made without sound of "saw or hammer."

Hate, envy, criticism, jealousy, competition, selfishness, war, suicide and murder are largely caused by acid conditions of the blood, producing changes by chemical poison and irritation of the brain cells, the keys upon which Soul plays "Divine Harmonies" or plays "fantastic tricks before high Heaven," according to the arrangement of chemical molecules in the wondrous laboratory of the soul.

Without a proper balance of the alkaline salt, the agent of peace and love, man is fit for "treason, stratagem and spoils." The chemistry of life points to the reason why man is unbalanced. Poise of tissue, nerve fluid, blood and brain cells, as well as muscular fibre, are conditions precedent to mental or soul poise. A man thinks and acts according to the organism in or through which the Ego operates.

The basis of the human body are twelve minerals, lime, iron, potash, silica, sodium, magnesia, etc., etc. They are found in the ashes of a cremated body, or, in reality, constitute the ashes. Before man ceases to be sick, before envy, strife, hatred, com- petition, selfishness, war and murder cease on earth, man must build his body on a plan that will express mind on the plane of altruism and love.

The perfectly balanced body will enable mind to cognize one- ness of being. From this concept comes peace on earth and good-will between man and man.

The knowledge of Life Chemistry will bring man to his Divine estate in the Kingdom of Harmony and Love. This Kingdom is forming in the chemicalizing mass of God's creative compounds. Out from the chemistry of elements, principles, monads and molecules; out of oxygen, hydrogen, nitrogen, carbon, helium, uranium, radium, aurium, argentum, sodium, potassium and iron—out from molecules composing the body of universal energy, a man and woman will be born—real Sons of God—who will bear away the sins of the world.

LESSON XI.

Sulphate of Soda.

Synonyms—Natrum Sulphate, Sodium Sulphuricum, Sodae or Sodii Sulphas, Glauber's Salts.

Formula—$Na_2 SO_4 10 H_2O$.

This may be obtained by the action of Sulphuric acid on sodium chloride (common salt).

This cell-salt is found in the intercellular fluids, liver and pancreas. Its principal work is to regulate the supply of water in the human organism.

The blood becomes overcharged with water, either from the oxidation of organic matter or from inhaling air that contains more aqueous vapor (water) than is required to produce normal blood. This condition of air is liable to prevail whenever the temperature is above 70 degrees.

One molecule of nat. sulph. has the power, chemical intelligence, to take up and carry away two molecules, or twice its bulk, of water. The blood does not become over charged with water from water taken into the stomach, but from the water lifted by expansion caused by heat above 70 degrees and held in the air and thus breathed into the arteries through the lungs. By the above we see that there is more work for this salt in hot weather than during cold weather. So-called malaria, Latin for bad air, is due to a lack of this tissue salt. Water, lifted from swamps or clear streams or lakes by the action of the sun's heat, is the same, for heat does not evaporate and lift poisonous, disintegrating organic matter from a swamp or marsh, but the water only.

Therefore, it is not some impurity in the air that causes chills, etc., but an oversupply of water which thins the bile and distributes it through the organism. Nature's effort to get rid of the surplus water by nervous, muscular and vascular contraction, on the principle of wringing water from a cloth, causes the spasm called chills. Proof of this theory is found in the fact that perspiration follows the chill. It generally requires about forty-eight hours to again overcharge the blood and bring on another chill.

Cold dry air always cures chills, and be it known that all cold air is dry air. The cure for chills when cold air cannot be had is sodium sulphate in biochemic potency. Yellow fever is caused by too much water in bile and other liver fluids. These fluids are distributed through the system, and in their union with oil, albumen, etc., become vitiated and cause the yellow skin.

Sodium Sulph. in crude form, is known as Glauber's Salts, and is too coarse to be taken up by the mucous membrane ab- sorbents and carried into the circulation; it must be triturated with sugar of milk, according to the biochemic method, up to the 3d or 6th decimal before using a remedy to supply the blood. Glauber's Salts, crude sodium sulphate, acts as a cathartic, and cathartics are never used in the biochemic system of healing.

When man learns to keep his blood at the proper rate of motion by the proper dynamos—the mineral salts—he will not fear fevers, microbes, mosquitoes, nor devils.

LESSON XII.

Silica.

Synonyms—Silica, silic, oxide, white pebble or common quartz. Chemical abbrevitaion, Si.

Made by fusing crude silica with carbonate of soda ; dissolve the residue, filter and precipitate by hydro-chloride acid.

This product must be triturated as per biochemic process before using internally.

This salt is the surgeon of the human organism. Silica is found in hair, skin, nails, periosteum, the membrane covering and protecting bone, the nerve sheath, called neurilemma, and a trace is found in bone tissue. The surgical qualities of silica lie in the fact that its particles are sharp cornered. A piece of quartz is a sample of the finer particles. Reduce silica to an impalpable powder and the microscope reveals the fact that the molecules are still pointed and jagged like a large piece of quartz rock. In all cases where it becomes necessary that decaying organic matter be discharged from any part of the body by the process of suppuration, these sharp pointed particles are pushed by the marvelous intelligence which operates without ceasing, day and night, in the wondrous human Beth, and like a lancet cuts a passage to the surface for the discharge of pus. Nowhere in all the records of physiology or biological research can anything be found more wonderful than the chemical and mechanical operation of this Divine artisan.

The bone covering is made strong and firm by silica. In case of boils or anthrax carbuncle, the biochemist loses no time searching for "anthrax bacilli," or germs, nor does he experiment with imaginary germ-killing serum, but simply furnishes nature with tools with which the necessary work may be accomplished.

Silica gives the glossy finish to hair and nails. A stalk of corn or straw of wheat, oats or barley would not stand upright except they contained this mineral.

THE COMING MAN

Out of the chemicalizing mass, out of the chemistry of elements, principles, minerals and monads—out of oxygen, hydrogen, nitrogen, carbon, helium, uranium, radium, arum, argentum, potassium sodium and iron—out from these molecules composing the substance of God a new man will be born, a real Son of God who will bear away the sins of the world. I see this form—physical body materializing out of the fomentation of life's creative compounds.

Now hasten, vibration from Uranus, and vitalize the Etheric Substance that sweeps through the rivers of Eden—the veins and arteries that carry the red cells of omnipresent life. Touch with thy fingers of fire, Golden Haired Apollo, the keys of the new man's wondrous brain until every atom and fiber of the holy temple joins in the Anthem of the stars. And Neptune, thou planet of Realization; at last thy hour has struck. Patient as the Divine Mother, thou hast waited for the man.

Lift thy Trident, O Trinity of Life, Liberty and Love, and send to Earth thy pent up vibrations of glory

Lo; theAquariusAge;—The new Heaven and new Earth;— The Co-operative Commonwealth;—The Brotherhood of man.

THE END

THE TREE OF LIFE

An Expose of Physical Regenesis on the Three-fold Plane of
Bodily, Chemical and Spiritual Operation.

BY GEORGE W. CAREY

INTRODUCTION

WHAT JEHOVAH, EVE, DAVID AND JOHN SAY

"And Jehovah God commanded the man saying,
Of every tree in the garden thou mayest freely eat: but of the tree of the knowledge of good and evil, thou shalt not eat of it, for the day that thou eatest thereof, thou shalt surely die.
"And the woman said unto the serpent, 'Of the fruit of the trees of the garden we may eat: but of the fruit of the tree which is in the midst of the garden, God hath said, Ye shall not eat of it, neither shall ye touch it, lest ye die."—*Gen. 1:16.*
"And he shall be like a tree planted by the streams of water,
"That bringeth forth its fruit in its Season, whose leaf also does not wither,
"And whatsoever he doeth shall prosper."—*David in Psalm I.*
"And on this side of the river and on that was the tree of life bearing twelve manner of fruits, yielding its fruit every month: And the leaves of the tree were for the healing of the Nations."—*John the Revelator, Chapt. 22.*

PART ONE

WONDERS AND POSSIBILITIES
OF THE HUMAN BODY

The human race has been asleep, and has dreamed that property and money are the true wealth of a nation, sacrificing men, women and children to the chimerical idea that danced in visionary splendor through their brains. The result of this is to be seen in the uneasiness that prevails everywhere. But humanity is waking up, slowly but surely and beginning to realize that it, itself, is the most precious thing on earth.

The old-established statement that the individuals that make up the race are imperfect is no more true than that a pile of lumber is imperfect, that is to be afterward reformed or built into a house. As it is the carpenter's business to take the lumber, which is perfect as material, and build the house, so it is the legitimate work of spiritual man to take the perfect material everywhere present and build, by the perfect law of chemistry and mathematics, the perfected, harmonious human being, and with this material, employ the same law to build up society collectively.

It is a well-known physiological fact that the blood is the basic material of which the human body is continually builded. As is the blood, so is the body; as is the body, so is the brain; as is the brain, so is the quality of thought. As a man is builded, so thinks he.

According to the views of students of modern alchemy, the Bible both the Old and New Testaments are symbolical writings, based primarily upon this very process of body-building. The word Alchemy really means Fleshology. It is derived from Chem, an ancient Egyptian word, meaning flesh. The word Egypt also means flesh, or anatomy.

Alchemy, however, in its broader scope, means the science of solar rays. Gold may be traced to the Sun's rays. The word gold means solar essence. The transmutation of gold does not mean the process of making gold, but does mean the process of changing gold, solar rays, into all manner of materialized forms, vegetable, mineral, etc. The ancient alchemist studied the process of Nature in her operations from the volatile to the fixed, the fluid to the solid, the essence to the substance, or the abstract to the concrete, all of which may be summed up in the changing of spirit into matter. In reality, the alchemist did not try to do anything. He simply tried to search out nature's processes in order that he might comprehend her marvelous operations.

To be sure, language was used that to us seems symbolical and often contradictory, but it was not so intended, nor so at all in reality. We speak in symbols. If a man is in delirium, caused by alcohol in his brain-cells, we say he has"snakes in his boots." Of course, no one supposes that the words are to be taken literally. Yet if our civilization should be wiped out, and our literature translated after four or five thousand years, those who read our history might be puzzled to know what was meant by "snakes in his boots."

Again, it has been believed by most people that the words, "transmutation of base metals into gold," used by alchemists, referred to making gold. But a careful study of the Hebrew Cosmogony, and the Kabala, will reveal the fact that the alchemist always referred to solar rays when he used the word gold. "Base metals,"simply means matter, or basic.

The dissolving, or disintegration of matter, the combustion of wood or coal, seemed as wonderful to these philosophers as the growth of wood or the formation of coal or stone. So, the transmutation of base metals into gold simply meant the process of changing the fixed into the volatile, or the dematerialization of matter, either by heat or chemical process.

It is believed by modern students of alchemy that the books

of the Old and New Testaments are a collection of alchemical and astrological writings, dealing entirely with the wonderful operation of aerial elements (Spirit) in the human body, so fearfully and wonderfully made. The same authority is given for the statements, "Know ye not that your bodies are the temple of the living God" and "Come unto Me all ye that labor and are heavy laden and I will give ye rest." According to the method of reading the numerical value of letters by the Kabala, M and E figure B, when united. Our B is from the Hebrew Beth, meaning a house or temple—the temple of the soul—the body. Thus by coming into the realization that the body is really the Father's House, temple of God, the soul secures peace and contentment or rest.

The human body is composed of perfect principles, gases, minerals, molecules, or atoms; but these builders of flesh and bone are not always properly adjusted. The planks or bricks used in building houses may be endlessly diversified in arrangement, and yet be perfect material.

Solomon's temple is an allegory of man's temple the human organism. This house is built (always being built) "without sound of saw or hammer."

The real Ego manifests in a house, beth, church, or temple— i. e., Soul-of-Man's Temple.

The solar (soular) plexus is the great central Sun or dynamo on which the Subconscious Mind (another name for God) operates and causes the concept of individual consciousness. The brain of man is the Son of God, the mediator (medium) between the central dynamo and the Cosmic Ocean of Space. Thus digestion or combustion of food, circulation of blood, inbreathing the breath of life (aerial elements), is carried on by the co-operation of the Holy Trinity; God, the solar plexus; the Son, the brain; and the Holy (whole) Spirit, or air.

No wonder that the seers and alchemists of old declared that "Your bodies are the temple of the living God" and

"The kingdom of Heaven is within you." But man, blinded by selfishness, searches here and there, scours the heavens with his telescope, digs deep into earth, and dives into ocean's depths, in a vain search for the Elixir of Life that may be found between the soles of his feet and the crown of his head. Really our human body is a miracle of mechanism. No work of man can compare with it in accuracy of its process and the simplicity of its laws.

At maturity, the human skeleton contains about 165 bones, so delicately and perfectly adjusted that science has despaired of ever imitating it.

The muscles are about 500 in number; length of alimentary canal, 32 feet; amount of blood in average adult, 30 pounds, or one-fifth the weight of the body; the heart is six inches in length and four inches in diameter, and beats seventy times per minute, 4200 times per hour, 100,800 per day, 36,720,000 per year. At each beat, two and one-half ounces of blood are thrown out of it, 175 ounces per minute, 656 pounds per hour, or about eight tons per day.

All the blood in the body passes through the heart every three minutes; and during seventy years it lifts 270,000,000 tons of blood.

The lungs contain about one gallon of air at their usual degree of inflation. We breathe, on an average, 1200 breaths per hour; inhale 600 gallons of air, or 24,000 gallons daily.

The aggregate surface of air-cells of the lungs exceed 20,000 square inches, an area nearly equal to that of a room twelve feet square. The average weight of the brain of an adult is three pounds, eight ounces; the average female brain, two pounds, four ounces. The convolutions of a woman's brain-cells and tissues are finer and more delicate in fibre and mechanism, which evidently accounts for the intuition of women. It would appear that the difference in the convolutions and fineness of tissue in brain matter is responsible for the degrees of consciousness called reason and intuition.

The nerves are all connected with the brain directly, or by the spinal marrow, but nerves receive their sustenance from the blood, and their motive power from the solar plexus dynamo. The nerves, together with the branches and minute ramifications, probably exceed ten millions in numbers.

The skin is composed of three layers, and varies from one-eighth to one-quarter of an inch in thickness. The average area of skin is estimated to be about 2000 square inches. The atmospheric pressure, being fourteen pounds to the square inch, a person of medium size is subject to a pressure of 40,000 pounds. Each square inch of skin contains 3500 sweat tubes, or perspiratory pores (each of which may be likened to a little drain tile) one-fourth of an inch in length, making an aggregate length of the entire surface of the body 201,166 feet, or a tube for draining the body nearly forty miles in length.

Our body takes in an average of five and a half pounds of food and drink each day, which amounts to one ton of solid and liquid nourishment annually, so that in seventy years a man eats and drinks 1000 times his own weight.

There is not known in all the realms of architecture or mechanics one little device which is not found in the human organism. The pulley, the lever, the inclined plane, the hinge, the "universal joint," tubes and trap-doors; the scissors, grind-stone, whip, arch, girders, filters, valves, bellows, pump, camera, and Aeolian harp; and irrigation plant, telegraph and telephone systems—all these and a hundred other devices which man thinks he has invented, but which have only been telegraphed to the brain from the Solar Plexus (cosmic centre) and crudely copied or manifested on the objective canvas.

No arch ever made by man is as perfect as the arch formed by the upper ends of the two legs and the pelvis to support the weight of the trunk. No palace or cathedral ever built has been provided with such a perfect system of arches and girders.

No waterway on earth is so complete, so commodious, or so populous as that wonderful river of life, the "Stream of Blood." The violin, the trumpet, the harp, the grand organ, and all the other musical instruments, are mere counterfeits of the human voice.

Man has tried in vain to duplicate the hinges of knee, elbow, fingers and toes, although they are a part of his own body.

Another marvel of the human body is the self-regulation process by which nature keeps the temperature in health at 98 degrees. Whether in India,

with the temperature at 130 degrees, or in the arctic regions, where the records show 120 degrees below the freezing point, the temperature of the body remains the same, practically steady at 98 degrees, despite the extreme to which it is subjected.

It was said that "all roads lead to Rome." Modern science has discovered that all roads of real knowledge lead to the human body. The human body is an epitome of the universe; and when man turns the mighty searchings of reason and investigation within that he has so long used without the New Heaven and Earth will appear.

While it is true that flesh is made by a precipitation of blood, it is not true that blood is made from food. The inorganic or cell-salts contained in food are set free by the process of combustion or digestion, and carried into the circulation through the delicate absorbent tubes of the mucous membrane of stomach and intestines. Air, or Spirit, breathed into the lungs, enters the arteries (air carriers) and chemically unites with the mineral base, and by a wonderful transformation creates flesh, bone, hair, nails, and all the fluids of the body.

On the rock (Peter or Petra, meaning stone) of the mineral salts is the human structure built, and the grave, stomach, or hell shall not prevail against it. The minerals in the body do not disintegrate or rot in the grave.

The fats, albumen, fibrine, etc., that compose the organic part of food, are burned up in the process of digestion and transposed into energy or force to run the human battery. Blood is made from air ; thus all nations that dwell on earth are of one blood, for all breathe one air. The best food is the food that burns up quickest and easiest; that is, with the least friction in ths human furnace.

The sexual functions of man and woman ; the holy operation of creative energy manifested in male and female ; the formation of life germs in ovum and sex fluids; the Divine Procedure of the "word made flesh" and the mysteries of conception and birth are the despair of science.

"Know ye not that your bodies are the temple of the living God?" for "God breathed into man the breath of life."

In the words of Epictitus, "Unhappy man, thou bearest a god about with thee, and knowest it not."

Walt Whitman sings :

"I loaf and invite my soul; I lean and loaf at my ease, observing a spear of summer grass. Clear and sweet is my soul, and clear and sweet is all that is not my soul."

"Welcome every organ and attribute of me, and of any man hearty and clean, not an inch, not a particle of an inch, is vile, and none shall be less familiar than the rest."

"Divine am I, inside and out, and I make holy whatever I touch or am touched from."

"I say no man has ever yet been half devout enough; none has ever yet adored or worshipped half enough; none has begun to think how divine he himself is, and how certain the future is."

The vagus nerve, so named because of its wandering (vagrant) branches, is the greatest marvel of the human organism. Grief depresses the circulation, through the vagus, a condition of malnutrition follows, and tuberculosis, often of the hasty type, follows.

The roots of the vagus nerve are in the medulla oblongata, at the base of the small brain or cerebellum, and explains why death follows the severing of the medulla. It controls the heart action, and if a drug such as aconite be administered, even in small doses, its effect upon this nerve is shown in slowing the action of the heart and decreasing the blood pressure. In larger doses it paralyzes the ends of the vagus in the heart, so that the pulse becomes suddenly very rapid and at the same time irregular. Branches of the vagus nerve reach the heart, lungs, stomach, liver and kidneys.

Worry brings on kidney disease, but it is the vagus nerve, and especially that branch running to the kidneys which under undue excitement or worry, or strain, brings about the paralysis of the kidneys in the performance of their functions.

When we say that a man's heart sinks within him for fear or apprehension, it is shown by the effect of this nerve upon the heart action. If his heart beats high with hopes, or he sighs for relief, it is the vagus nerve that has conducted the mental state to the heart and accelerated its action or caused that spasmodic action of the lungs which we call a sigh.

The nerves of the human body constitute the "Tree of Life," with its leaves of healing. The flowing waters of the Rivers of Life are the veins and arteries through which sweep the red, magnetic currents of Love—of Spirit made visible.

> Acids and alkalis acting,
>   Proceeding and acting again,
> Operating, transmuting, fomenting,
>   In throes and spasms of pain—
> Uniting, reacting, atoning,
>   Like souls passing under the rod—
> Some people call it Chemistry,
>   Others call it GOD.

Behold the divine telegraph system, the million nerve wires running throughout the wondrous temple, the temple not made with hands, the temple made "without sound of saw or hammer." View the Central Sun of the human system—the Solar Plexus—vibrating life abundantly.

Around this dynamo of God, you may see the Beasts that worship before the Throne day and night

saying, "Holy, holy, art Thou, Lord God Almighty." The Beasts are the twelve plexuses of nerve centers, telegraph stations, like unto the twelve zodiacal signs that join hands in a fraternal circle across the gulf of space.

Aviation, liquified air, deep breathing for physical development and the healing of divers diseases rule the day. In every brain there are dormant cells, waiting for the "coming" of the bridegroom, the vibration of the air age (the Christ) that will resurrect them.

Everywhere we have evidence of the awakening of dormant brain cells. Much, if not all, of spiritual phenomena, multiple personality, mental telepathy, and kindred manifestations, are explainable upon the hypothesis of the possibility of awakening and bringing into use of dormant brain cells.

The eye is hardly less wonderful, being a perfect photographer's camera. The retina is the dry plate on which are focused all objects by means of the crystalline lens. The cavity behind this lens is the shutter. The eyelid is the drop shuttle. The draping of the optical dark room is the only black membrane in the entire body. This miniature camera is self-focusing, self-loading and self-developing, and takes millions of pictures every day in colors and enlarged to life size.

Charts have been prepared—marvelous charts—which go to show that the eye has 729 distinct expressions conveying us many distinct shades of meaning.

The power of color perception is overwhelming. To perceive red the retina of the eye must receive 395,000 vibrations in a second; for violet it must respond to 790,000,000. In our waking moments our eyes are bombarded every minute by at least 600,000,000 vibrations.

The ear is a colossal mystery, and the phenomenon of sound is a secret only recorded in the Holy of Holies of the Infinite Mind. And what is mind? We know absolutely nothing about it. Some believe that mind is the product of the chemical operation of matter, viz.: the atoms or materials that compose the human body. These persons contend that all electrons are particles of pure Intelligence and know what to do. Others hold to the theory that universal Mind (whatever it may be) forms a body from some material, they know not what, and then plays upon it or operates through it.

> Visions of beauty and splendor,
>   Forms of a long-lost race,
> Sounds and faces and voices
>   From the fourth dimension of space ;
> And on through the universe boundless,
>   Our thoughts go, lightning-shod ;
> Some call it Imagination,
>   And others call it God !

We wonder and adore in the presence of that puls- ing orb, the heart. Tons of the water of life made red by the Chemistry of Love sweep through this central throne every day, and flow on to enrich the Edenic Garden until its waste places shall bloom and blossom as the rose.

Take my hand and go with me to the home of the Soul that wonderful brain. Can you count the whirling, electric, vibrating cells ? No, not until you can count the sand grain on the ocean's shore. These rainbow-hued cells are the keys that the fingers of the soul strike to play its part in the Symphony of the Spheres.

At last we have seen the "Travail of the Soul and are satisfied." No more temples of the Magi now, but instead the Temple of the Ego, the glorious human Beth. At least we have found the true church of God, the human body. In this body, or church, spirit operates like some wizard chemist or electrician. No more searching through India's jungles or scaling the Himalayan heights in search for a master—a mahatma—or ancient priest dwelling in some mysterious cave where occult rites and ceremonies are supposed to reveal the wisdom of the past. But instead, you have found the Kingdom of the Real within the Temple that needs no outer Sun by day nor Moon nor Stars by night to lighten it. And then the enraptured Soul becomes conscious that the stone has been rolled away from the door of material concept where it has slept, and it now hears the voice of the Father within saying, "Let there be light!" and feels the freedom that comes with knowing that Being is one.

And now, man, the Ego, also realizes the meaning of the "Day of Judgment." It realizes that Judgment means understanding, hence the ability to judge. Man then judges correctly, for he sees the Wisdom of Infinite Life in all men, in all things, all events, and all environments. Thus does the new birth take place, and the Kingdom of Harmony reigns now. Man must realize, however, that he is the creator or builder of his own body, and that he is responsible for every moment of its building, and every hour of its care. He alone can select and put together the materials provided by the universe for its construction. Man has been able to scale the heavens, to measure the distances between the stars and planetary bodies, and to analyze the component parts of suns and worlds, yet he cannot eat without making himself ill; he can foretell eclipses and tides for years in advance, but cannot look far enough ahead in his own affairs to say when he may be brought down with la grippe, or to calculate accurately the end of any bodily ill that may afflict him. When he finds out what he really is, and how much he has always had to do in the making of himself what he is, he will be ready to grasp some idea of the wonderful possibilities of every human soul and body, and will know how completely and entirely is every man his own savior. Just so long as he denies his own powers, and looks outside of himself for salvation from present or future ills, he is indeed a lost creature. If the race is to be redeemed, it must come as the result of thought followed by action. If the race is to think differently than at present, it must have new bodies with new brains. Man must be born again.

Modern physiologists know that our bodies are completely made over every year, by the throwing off of worn-out cells and the formation of new ones, that is going on every minute. Nature will take care of the making-over process, but we are responsible for the plan of reconstruction. Man must learn to run the machinery of his body with the same mathematical accuracy as he now displays in control of an engine or automobile, before he can lay claim to his divine heritage and proclaim himself master of his own.

The law of life is not a separate agent working independently of mankind and separate from individual life. Man himself is a phase of the great law in operation. When he once fully awakens to the universal co-operation of the attributes and thoughts through which the great dynamis operates or proceeds, he—the Ego—one of the expressions of infinity, will be enabled to free himself from the seeming environments of matter, and thus realizing his power, will assert his dominion over all he has been an agent in creating. And he has indeed assisted in creating—manifesting—all that is. Being a thought, an outbreathing of universal spirit, he is co-eternal with it.

In material concept, we do not begin to realize the extent of our wisdom. When we awaken to spirit, consciousness knowledge that we are egos that have bodies or temples, and not bodies that have souls, or spirits, we see the object or reason of all symbols or manifestation, and begin to realize our own power over all created things.

And in this Aquarian age, great changes in nature's laws will be speedily brought to pass, and great changes in the affairs of humanity will result. The laws of vibration will be mastered, and through their operation material manifestations will be shaped and moulded to man's will. It is only a matter of time when all the necessities of life will be produced directly from the elements of the air.

It is well known by chemists that all manner of fruits, grains and vegetables are produced directly from the elements in air, and not from soil. The earth, of course, serves as a negative pole and furnishes the mineral salts of lime, magnesium, iron, potassium, sodium and silica, which act as carriers of water, oil, fibrin, sugar, etc., and thus build up the

plant; but oil, sugar, albumin, etc., are formed by a precipitation or condensation of principles in air, and not from soil. This is a fact abundantly proved. Mr. Berthelot, a scientist of France, Tesla, the Austrian wizard, and our own Edison have long held that food can be produced by a synthetic process from its elements artificially.

Some six or seven extracts, as well as coloring material, are now being manufactured in this manner. Madder is made almost exclusively by this process now.

Sugar has recently been made in the laboratory from glycerin, which Professor Berthelot first made direct from synthetic alcohol. Commerce has now taken up the question; and an invention has been patented by which sugar is to be made upon a commercial scale, from two gases, at something like 1 cent per pound. M. Berthelot declares he has not the slightest doubt that sugar will eventually be manufactured on a large scale synthetically, and that the culture of sugar cane and beet root will be abandoned, because they have ceased to pay.

The chemical advantages promised by M. Berthelot to future generations are marvelous. He cites the case of alzarin, a compound whose synthetic manufacture by chemists has destroyed a great agricultural industry. It is the essential commercial principle of the madder root, which was once used in dyeing. The chemists have now succeeded in making pure indigo direct from its elements, and it will soon be a commercial product. Then the indigo fields, like the madder fields, will be abandoned, industrial laboratories having usurped their place.

Biochemists long ago advanced the theory that animal tissue is formed from the air inhaled, and not from food. The food, of course, serves its purpose; it acts as the negative pole, as does the earth to plant and vegetable life, and also furnishes the inorganic salts, the workers that carry on the chemistry of life, setting free magnetism, heat and electric forces by disintegration and fermentation of the organic portions of the food.

But air, in passing through the various avenues and complex structure of the human organism, changes, condenses, solidifies, until it is finally deposited as flesh and bone. From this established scientific truth, it appears that, by constructing a set of tubes, pumps, etc., resembling the circulatory system, as well as the lung cells of the human mechanism, which is a chemical laboratory, where the chemistry of spirit is ever at work, changing the one essence of spirit substance to blood, flesh and bone, air may be changed into an albuminous pabulum, which may be again changed into the special kind of food required by adding the proper flavor, which may also be produced direct from the air.

There does not seem to be any reason why this substance, the basis of all food or vegetable growth, cannot, by proper process, be made into material for clothing. Wool, cotton, flax, silks, etc., are all produced from the universal elements through the slow, laborious and costly process of animal or vegetable growth. Why not produce them direct?

Those who believe in a time of peace on earth, a millennial reign, certainly do not think that our present mode of producing food will continue during that age. Slaughter of animals, and fruit, grain or vegetable raising leave small time for men and women to enjoy a condition foretold by all the seers and prophets. But under the new way of producing food and clothing, the millennium is possible.

And thus will the problem of subsistence be solved. No more monopoly of nature's bounties. An exchange of service will be the coin of the world instead of certain metals difficult to obtain.

A realization of this vision, or theory, that will for awhile be called visionary by most people, will mean Eden restored. The Earth will be allowed to return to its natural state. We will cease to eat animals birds and fishes. Many people have wondered why, during the last few years fruit pests have multiplied so alarmingly, and why cows are almost universally diseased and so much attention given to meat, milk, and butter products by Boards of Health, etc. There is surely a reason. The One Life, Supreme Intelligence, or Divine Wisdom, that holds the worlds of space in their appointed orbits, surely knows all about the affairs of earth. When a new dispensation is about to be ushered in, old things begin to pass away.

All labor, preparing food and clothing, as now carried on, will cease, and the people, in governmental or collective capacity, will manufacture and distribute all manner of food and clothing free. Machinery for the production of everything necessary for man's material wants will be simple and easily manipulated. One-twentieth of the able-bodied population, working one or two hours a day, and shifting every week, or day, for that matter, with others, will produce an abundant supply. Neither droughts nor floods nor winter's snow can affect the supply. It can be made in Klondyke or the Tropics. Garments may be worn for a few days and then burned, and laundry work cease. Cooking will be reduced to a minimum. No preparing vegetables, fruit or cracking nuts; no making butter, or preserving meats. Men will not have to devote their lives to the endless grind of food production, nor women to cooking, dish-washing, sewing, and laundry-work. Garments of beautiful design and finest texture will be made by machines invented for the purpose, ready for wear.

A dream, you say? I cannot admit that in the fact of the indisputable evidence already produced: but what if it were, at present, but the dream it may appear to the one who hears of its methods of operation for the first time? Do dreams ever come true? Yea, verily? All concrete facts are materialized dreams.

An Egyptian King dreamed, and the Pyramids of Cheops mass and miracle his vision. The Pyramids are encyclopedic of physical science and astral lore. The science of numbers, weights, measures, geometry astronomy, astrology, and all the deeper mysteries of the human body and soul are embodied in these incomparable monuments.

A dream of an ancient alchemist solidified in stone, and the awful sphinx sat down in Egypt's sand to gaze into eternity.

Columbus dreamed, and a white-sailed ship turned its prow west and west. On unchartered seas, with an eternity of water ahead, he remembered his dream, and answered "Sail on!" to the discouraged mate, until he landed on the unknown shores of a most wonderful new world.

Michael Angelo dreamed a thousand dreams and sleeping marble awoke and smiled. Hudson and Fulton dreamed, and steamboats "run over and under the seas."

The Pilgrim Fathers dreamed and America, the "marvel of nations" banners the skies with the stars and stripes. Marcus Whitman and Lewis and Clarke dreamed long and hard and the bones of oxen and men and women and babies made a bridge over the desert sands and the mountain gorges to the shores of the Sundown Sea, and now the Pullman cars come safely over. Morse and Marconi and Edison dreamed strange wild dreams and concentrated intelligence springs from carbon-crucible and says to earth's boundaries, "Lo; here am I."

Vibration of etheric substance
   Causing light through regions of space,
A girdle of something enfolding
   And binding together the race—
And words without wires transmitted,
   Aerial-winged, spirit-sandalled and shod:
Some call it electricity,
   And others call it God!

A mechanic dreamed, and sprang upon his automobile, and drove it till the axles blazed and the spaces shriveled behind him. Men of high strung airy brains dreamed wondrous dreams, and now the eagle's highway and the open road to men lie parallel.

A musician dreamed a sweet, harmonious dream, and forth from a throat of brass and discs of carbon directed by a million tiny fingers of steel, came the entrancing notes that had run riot through the singer's brain.

So let us dream on, men and women, of the day of rest that is already dawning in the heavens. No wonder that Paul said: "Now, brethren, are we the Sons of God, but it doth not yet appear what we shall be as such. The morning light of that glad day now purples the mountains of faith and hope with its rays of glory.

And when Man is once fully alive to his own heritage, realizing the wonders and possibilities of his own body, and to provide for its needs, he will assert the divine right within him to be an Ego, a soul, in command of its own temple, and the environments of that temple, and will rejoice in the revealed truth of his own divinity that alone can make him free.

PART TWO

THE BRIDGE OF LIFE

"A noiseless, patient spider,
I mark'd, where, on a little promontory, it stood, isolated;
Mark'd how, to explore the vacant, vast surrounding,
It launch'd forth filament, filament, filament, out of itself;
Ever unreeling them—ever tirelessly speeding them.

"And you, O my soul, where you stand,
Surrounded, surrounded, in measureless oceans of space,
Ceaselessly musing, venturing, throwing—seeking the spheres,
            to connect them;
Till the bridge you will need, be form'd—till the ductile
            anchor hold ;
Till the gossamer thread you fling, catch somewhere, O my soul."

—WALT WHITMAN

The statement by Holy Writ that "man is conceived in sin and brought forth in iniquity" has a threefold meaning, viz., chemical, physiological, and astrological. The translation from the Hebrew text as given is crude and misleading. The real meaning in the original is, that the human embryo remains nine months in the female laboratory, thus falling short three months of completing a solar year, or soul year. Twelve represents a complete circle.

The word sin comes from Schin, the 21st letter of the Hebrew alphabet, and means to fall short of completeness or understanding. In the Tarot symbol, S, or Sin, is represented by the "Blind Fool," one lacking in wisdom. "Brought forth in iniquity" is merely a repetition of the words "born in sin." Iniquity and inequity, or unequal, mean the same. The ancient Hebrews called Moon, Sin, because it gave light only part of the time.

To acquire wisdom that will enable the Ego in flesh to build a bridge across the three-month gap, or space between the point of conception and birth, is the one real problem that confronts Soul on the material plane of expression. The alchemists, seers, and astrologians of all ages have wrestled with this problem in their ceaseless endeavors to unravel the great mystery of man's dominion over flesh. Whether it be the chemist seeking new compounds, the physiologist searching and testing the fluids of the fearfully and wonderfully made body of man, or the alchemist probing for the Elixir of Life—the Ichor of the Gods—or the astrologian pulling and adjusting the etheric wires that criss-cross the spaces in an earnest desire to make good and sane the statement "The wise man rules his stars,"—all, all are seeking to span the awful space that yawns between the neophyte and the Promised Land of immortality in the body, where "in my flesh I shall see God," and when and where he can truly say with the regenerated Job, "I have heard of thee by the hearing of the ear, but now mine eye seeth thee." Man must workout his own salvation.

The bridge to be built across the three-months space must have a mineral base or rock foundation. "Thou are Peter (petra, stone, or mineral), on thee will I build my church," etc. Church is from the second Hebrew letter, Beth, a house, temple, or church. The human body is a house, temple, or church for Soul. "Know ye not that your bodies are the temple (church) of God?"

There are twelve inorganic mineral cell-salts in the human body, and these minerals (stones in the temple) correspond in vibration to the twelve signs of the Zodiac. During the nine months of gestation the embryo receives and appropriates the creative energies of nine of these salts, leaving three to be supplied after the parting of the umbilical cord. Take for example a native born February 22nd, with the Sun's entry into Pisces: The embryo having begun its journey at the gate of Gemini and negotiated the nine gestatory signs, his blood vibration at birth is thus deficient in the qualities of Pisces, Aries and Taurus, as also in the chemical dynamics of phosphate of iron, phosphate of potassium, and sulphate of sodium—the mineral bases respectively of the signs of this uncompleted quadrant. In so far as his circulatory system may receive these needed builders, health will be balanced and life prolonged.

The chemical union of these cell-salts with organic matter, such as oil, fibrin, albumen, etc., forms the various tissues of the body, and administers to the physiological needs as represented by the Bridge, that the multiple cells may respond more harmoniously and completely to the magic touch of the Divine energy, just as the tones of a musical instrument are made the more melodious through a properly skilled manipulation. And as bridge-building in a mechanical sense depends upon the plans and specifications of a competent civil engineer, so does the Bridge of Life depend upon the astrologian to chart and compass the way.

Our diagram indicates at a glance the chemical formulae that appertain respectively to the zodiacal divisions, but to give a clearer conception as regards their specific qualities and physiological action in relation to the various signs, reference may be had to the following compend :

ARIES : From the teachings of the Chemistry of Life we find that the basis of brain or nerve fluid is a certain mineral salt known as potassium phosphate, or Kali Phos.

The Phosphate of Potash.

Synonyms : Potassium Phosphate, Kali Phosphoricum, Potassii Phosphas.

Formula : K_2HPO_4 .

It may be prepared by mixing aqueous phosphoric acid with a sufficient quantity of potash, hydrate or carbonate, until the reaction is slightly alkaline and evaporating. Triturate to 3d or 6th X.

This salt is the great builder of the positive brain cells. Kali phos. unites with albumen and by some subtle alchemy transmutes it and forms gray brain matter.

When the chemical possibilities of this brain builder are fully understood insane asylums will go out of fashion.

Man has been deficient in understanding because his brain receiver did not vibrate to certain subtle influences; the dynamic cells in the gray matter of nerve were not finely attuned and did not respond—hence sin, or falling short of understanding.

TAURUS: Sulphate of Soda.

Synonyms: Natrum Sulphate, Sodium Sulphuricum, Sodae or Sodii Sulphas, Glauber's Salts.

Formula $Na_2 (SO_4—10H_2O)$.

May be obtained by the action of Sulphuric acid on sodium chloride (common salt).

This cell-salt is found in the intercellular fluids, liver and pancreas. Its principal work is to regulate the supply of water in the human organism.

The blood becomes overcharged with water, either from the oxidation of organic matter or from inhaling air that contains more aqueous vapor (water) than is required to produce normal blood. This condition of air is liable to prevail whenever the temperature is above 70 degrees.

One molecule of nat. sulph. has the power (chemical intelligence) to take up and carry away two molecules, or twice its bulk of water. The blood does not become overcharged with water from water taken into the stomach, but from the water lifted by expansion caused by heat above 70 degrees and held in the air and thus breathed into the arteries through the lungs. By the above we see that there is more work for this salt in hot weather than during cold weather. So-called malaria, Latin for bad air, is due to a lack of this tissue salt. Water lifted from swamps or clear streams or lakes by the action of the sun's heat is the same; for heat does not evaporate and lift poisonous disintegrating organic matter from a swamp or marsh, but the water only.

GEMINI : The Chloride of Potash, or Potassium.
Synonyms: Potassium chloride, Kali Muriaticum, Kali Chloratum, Kali Chloridum, Potassi Chloridum.
Formula: K Cl.
This salt must not be confused with the chlorate of potash, a poison, chemical formula $K ClO_3$.
Chloride of potash may be obtained by neutralizing pure aqueous hydrochloric acid with pure potassium carbonate or hydrate.
The cell-salt kali muriaticum (Potassium chloride) is the mineral worker of blood that forms fibrin and properly diffuses it through the tissues of the body.
Kali mur molecules are principal agents used in the chemistry of life to build fibrin into the human organism.
The skin that covers the face contains the lines and angles that give expression and thus differentiate one person from another.
In venous blood fibrin amounts to three in one thousand parts; when the molecules of Kali mur fall below the standard in the blood fibrin thickens, causing what is known as pleurisy, pneumonia, catarrh, diphtheria, etc. When the circulation fails to throw out the thickened fibrin via the glands or mucous membrane, it may stop the action of the heart. Em- bolus is a Latin word meaning little lump, or balls ; therefore to die of embolus, or "heart failure" generally means that the heart's action was stopped by little lumps of fibrin clogging the auricles and ventricles of the heart.

When the blood contains the proper amount of kali mur, fibrin is functional and the symptoms referred to above do not manifest.

CANCER : Fluoride of Lime.

Synonyms : Calcaria Flurica, Calcium Fluoride.

Chemical Formula : CaF_2 .

This salt is formed by the union of lime and fluorine.

The inorganic salts are the workers, controlled and directed by infinite intelligence, that performs the ceaseless miracle of creation or formation.

Biologists and physiologists have searched long and patiently for a solution to the mystery of the differentiation of material forms.

No ordinary test can detect any difference in the ovum of fish, reptile, bird, beast or man. Chemical analysis reveals the same mineral salts, carbon, oil, fibrine, albumen, sugar, etc., in the life cell, or ovum in the blood, tissue, hair, or bone of the multiple and varied expression of life in material forms.

The chemistry of life answers the "Riddle of the Sphinx," and writes above the temple door of investigation: "Let there be light." There is no such thing as dead or inert. All is life. A crystal is an aggregation of living organism. The base of all material manifestation is mineral. "Out of the dust (ashes or mineral) of earth physical man is made." The twelve mineral salts of lime, iron, potash, sodium, silica and magnesium are the foundation stones of every visible form of animal or vegetable. No two forms of the different species of animals have the same combination of this "rock foundation," but all have some of the same minerals.

It is quite as important for a student of Biochemistry to understand the process by which certain cell-salts operate to supply a deficiency as it is to know what a particular symptom calls for.

Elastic fibre, the chief organic substance in rubber, is formed by a chemical union of the fluoride of lime

with albumen, oil, etc. Therefore, we find this salt dominant in the elastic fibre of the body, in the enamel of teeth and connective tissue.

A lack of salt in proper amount causes relaxed condition of muscular tissue, falling of the womb and varicose veins. Sometimes there is a non-functional combination of this salt with oil and albumen which forms a solid deposit, causing swelling of stony hardness ; it is a sort of incomplete fibre with other lime salts and vitiated fluids of the body.

LEO: Phosphate of Magnesia.
Synonyms: Magnesium Phosphorica.
Formula: $MgHOPO_47(H_2O)$.

This cell-salt may be made by mixing Phosphate of Soda with Sulphate of Magnesia. This salt is found chiefly in the white fibres of nerves and muscles. The tissues of nerves and muscles are composed of many very fine threads or strands of different colors, each acting as a special telegraph wire, each one having a certain conductile power or quality, special chemical affinity for, certain organic substances, oil or albumen, through and by which the organism is materialized and the process or operations of life are carried on. The imagination might easily conceive the idea that these delicate infinitesimal fibres are strings of the Human Harp, and that molecular minerals are the fingers of infinite Energy striking notes of some Divine Anthem.

The white fibres of nerves and muscles need the

dynamic action of Magnesia Phosphate especially to keep them in proper tune, or function, for by its chemical action on albumen the special fluid for white nerve or muscle fibre is formed. When the supply of this salt falls below the standard, cramps, sharp shooting pains or some spasmodic condition prevails. Such symptoms are simply calls of nature for more magnesia.

The impulsive traits of Leo people are symboled
In the pulse, which is a reflex of heart throbs.

The phosphate of magnesia, in biochemic therapeutics, is the remedy for all spasmodic impulsive symptoms. This salt supplies the deficient worker or builder in such cases and thus restores normal conditions. A lack of muscular force, or nerve vigor, indicates a disturbance in the operation of the heart cell-salt, magnesia phosphate, which gives the "Lion's spring," or impulse.

VIRGO: Sulphate of Potash.
Synonyms : Potassium Sulphate, Kali Sulphos, Potassae Sulphos, Kali Sulphate.
Formula: K_2SO_4.

The microscope reveals the fact that, when the body is in health, little jets of steam are constantly escaping from the seven million pores of the skin.

The human body is a furnace and steam engine. The stomach and bowels burn food by chemical operation as truly as the furnace of a locomotive consumes by combustion. In the case of the locomotive the burning of coal furnishes force which vibrates water and causes an expansion (rate of motion) that we name steam.

The average area of skin is estimated to be about 2,000 square inches. The atmospheric pressure being fourteen pounds to the square inch, a person of medium size is subject to a pressure of 40,000 pounds.

Each square inch of skin contains 3500 sweat tubes or perspiratory pores (each of which may be likened to a little drain tile) one-fourth of an inch in length, making an aggregate length of the entire surface of the body 201,166 feet, or a tile draining for the body nearly forty miles in length.

All tangible elements are the effects of certain rates of motion on the intangible and unseen elements. Nitrogen gas is mineral in solution, or ultimate potency.

Oil is made by the union of the sulphate of potassium (potash) with albuminoids and aerial elements. The first element that is disturbed in the organism of those born in the celestial sign Virgo is oil; this break in the function of oils shows a deficiency in potassium sulphate, known in pharmacy as kali sulph. Virgo is represented in the human body by the stomach and bowels, the laboratory in which food is consumed as fuel to set free the minerals, in order that they may enter the blood through the mucous membrane absorbents.

The letter X in Hebrew is Samech or Stomach. X or cross, means crucifixion, or charge, transmutation.

LIBRA : Phosphate of Soda.

Synonyms: Natrum Phosphate, Sodium Phosphate, Phosphos Natricus, Sodae Phosphate.

Formula: Na_2HPO_4 ;$12H_2O$.

This alkaline cell-salt is made from bone ash or by neutralizing orthophosphoric acid with carbonate of sodium.

Sodium, or natrum, phosphate holds the balance between acids and normal fluids of the human body.

Acid is organic and can be chemically split into two or more elements, thus destroying the formula that makes the chemical rate of motion called acid.

Acid conditions are not due to an excess of acid in the blood, bile or gastric fluids. Supply the alkaline salt sodium phosphate, and acid will chemically change to normal fluids.

A certain amount of acid is necessary, and always present in the blood, nerve, stomach and liver fluids. The apparent excess of acid is nearly always due to a deficiency in the alkaline, salt.

Acid, in alchemical lore, is represented as Satan (Saturn), while sodium phosphate symbolizes Christ (Venus). An absence of the Christ principle gives license to Satan to run riot in the Holy Temple. The Advent of Christ drives the thief out with a whip of thongs. Reference to temple in the figurative language of Bible and New Testament always symbols the human organism. "Know ye not that your bodies are the Temple of the living God?"

Solomon's temple is an allegory of the physical body of man and woman. Soul—of man's temple—the house, church, Beth or temple made without sound of "saw or hammer."

Hate, envy, criticism, jealousy, competition, selfishness, war, suicide and murder are largely caused by acid conditions of the blood producing changes upon which Soul plays "Divine Harmonies" or "fantastic tricks before high heaven," according to the arrangement of chemical molecules in the wondrous laboratory of the soul.

Without a proper balance of the alkaline salt, the agent of peace and love, man is fit for "treason, stratagem and spoils."

SCORPIO : Sulphate of Lime.
Synonyms: Calcium Sulphate, Calcarea Sulphate, Calc Sulphos, Gypsum, Plaster of Paris.
Formula: $CaSo_4$.
This salt can be obtained by precipitating a solution of chloride of lime with dilute sulphuric acid.

SAGITTARIUS : The mineral or cell-salt of blood corresponding to Sagittarius is Silica.
Synonyms: Silica, Silic, Oxide, White Pebble or Common Quartz. Chemical abbreviation, Si.
Made by fusing crude silica with carbonate of soda; dissolve the residue, filter, and precipitate by hydrochloric acid.
This product must be triturated as per biochemic process before using internally.
This salt is the surgeon of the human organism.

Silica is found in hair, skin, nails, periosteum, the membrane covering and protecting bone, the nerve sheath, called neurilemma, and a trace is found in bone tissue. The surgical qualities of silica lie in the fact that its particles are sharp cornered. A piece of quartz is a sample of the finer particles. Reduce silica to an inpalpable powder and the microscope reveals the fact that the molecules are still pointed and jagged like a large piece of quartz rock. In all cases where it becomes necessary that decaying organic matter be discharged from any part of the body by the process of suppuration, these sharp-pointed particles are pushed by the marvellous intelligence that operates without ceasing, day and night, in the wondrous human Beth, and like a lancet cut a passage to the surface for the discharge of pus. Nowhere in all the records of physiology or biological research can anything be found more wonderful than the chemical and mechanical operation of this Divine artisan.

The Centaur of mythology is known in the "Circles of Beasts that worship before the Lord (Sun) day and night," as Sagittarius, the Archer, with drawn bow. Arrow heads are composed of fiint, decarbonized white pebble or quartz. Thus we see why silica is the special birth salt of all born in the Sagittarius sign.

CAPRICORN :

Phosphate of Lime.

Synonyms: Calcerea Phosphoricum, Calcium Phosphate.

Formula: Ca_3Po_4.

Phosphoric acid dropped in lime water precipitates this salt. Circle means Sacrifice, according to the Cabala, the straight line bending to form a circle. Thus we find twelve zodiacal signs sacrificing to the sun. Twelve months sacrifice for a solar year. Twelve functions of man's body sacrifice for the temple, Beth, or "Church of God" the human house of flesh. Twelve minerals known as cell-salts sacrifice by operation and combining to build tissue. The dynamic force of these vitalized workmen constitutes the chemical affinities the positive and negative poles of mineral expression.

The Cabalistic numerical value of the letters g, o, a, t, add up 12.

AQUARIUS : Sodium Chloride.

Synonyms: Natrum Muriaticum, Sodii Chloridium, Chloruretum, Chloruretum of Sodicum, Common table salt. Must be triturated up to 3d decimal before it can be taken up by mucous membrane absorbants and carried into the circulation.

Formula: NaCe.

Air contains 78 per cent of nitrogen gas, believed by scientists to be mineral in ultimate potency. Minerals are formed by the precipitation of nitrogen gas. Differentiation is attained by the proportion of oxygen and aqueous vapor (hydrogen) that unites with nitrogen.

A combination of sodium and chlorine forms the mineral known as common salt. This mineral absorbs water. The circulation or distribution of water in the human organism is due to the chemical action of the molecules of sodium chloride.

Aquarius is known as "The Water Bearer." Sodium chloride, known also as natrum muriaticum, is also a bearer of water, and chemically corresponds with the zodiacal angle of Aquarius.

PISCES: Phosphate of Iron.

Synonyms: Ferrum Phosphate, Ferri Phosphas.

Formula: $Fe_3 (PO_4)^2$.

Phosphate of iron may be prepared by mixing sodium phosphate with sulphate of iron. The salt precipitated by this union is filtered, washed, dried and rubbed to a powder.

The iron phosphate should not be used below the sixth (decimal trituration), as large doses of iron, as in tinctures, have a bad effect on the mucous lining of the stomach, injure the teeth and utterly fail to supply iron to the blood where it is needed to carry oxygen, the life giver.

One red blood corpuscle does not exceed the one hundred and twenty millionth of a cubic inch. There are more than three million such cells in one drop of blood, and these cells carry the iron in the blood. How necessary, then, to administer the salts of iron to hungry cells in the most minute molecular form.

Each one of the twelve inorganic salts has its own sphere of function and curative action. Thus we find the phosphate of iron molecularly deficient in all fevers and inflammatory symptoms.

Health depends on a proper amount of iron phosphate in the blood, for the molecules of this salt have chemical affinity for oxygen and carry it to all parts of the organism. When these oxygen carriers are deficient, the circulation is increased in order to conduct a sufficient amount of oxygen to the extremities with the diminished quantity of iron, exactly as seven men must move faster to do the work of ten. This increased rate of motion of the blood is changed to heat, caused by friction, otherwise known as the "conservation of energy."

This heat, or increase in the temperature of blood, has been named fever, from the Latin word fervere, meaning "To boil out."

The writer fails to see any relevancy between the word fever and a deficiency in iron phosphate molecules in the blood. From Hippocrates to Koch you will not find a true definition of fever outside of the Biochemic theory.

It is not simply the heat that causes distress in a fever patient, but it is the lack of oxygen in the blood due to a deficiency in iron, the carrier of oxygen. The feet are the foundation of the body. Iron is the foundation of blood. Most diseases of Pisces people commence with symptoms indicating a deficiency of iron molecules in the blood; hence it is inferred that those born between the dates of February 19 and March 21 use more iron than do those born in other signs.

Iron is known as the magnetic mineral, due to the fact that it attracts oxygen. Pisces people possess great magnetic force "in their hands and make the best magnetic healers.

The astronomer, by the unerring law of mathematics applied to space, proportion, and the so far discovered wheels and cogs of the uni-machine, can tell where a certain planet must be located, before the telescope has verified the prediction. So the astro-biochemist knows there must of necessity be a blood mineral and tissue builder to correspond with each of the duodenary segments that constitute the circle of the Zodiac.

Not through quarantine, nor disinfectants, nor boards of health, will man reach the long-sought plane of physical well-being; nor by denials of disease will bodily regeneration be wrought; nor by dieting or fasting or "Fletcherizing" or suggesting, will the Elixir of Life and the Philosopher's Stone be found.

The Mercury of the Sages and the "hidden manna" are not constituents of health foods. Victims of salt baths and massages are bald before their time, and the alcohol, steam and Turkish bath fiends die young.

Only when man's body is made chemically perfect will the mind be able perfectly to express itself.

And the secret of this chemical perfectionment is the sum total of the requirements involved in this zodiacal Bridge. The rock Peter, or Petra must be perfectly formed before the etheric wires which span the gulf between birth forward to the sidereal point of conception can vibrate in such harmony as to sustain the traveller on this "magical bridge of three piers," or the three zodiacal signs through which the material body must successfully function before it may hope to lift the veil of Isis.

The Bridge of Life, a symbol of physical regenesis, has been exploited in song, drama, and story. Paracelsus, Pythagoras, Lycurgus, Valentin, Wagner, and a long and unbroken line of the Illuminati, from time immemorial have chanted their epics in unison with this "riddle of the Sphinx," across the scroll of which is written, "Solve me, or die."

Of all the multiple adepts or masters that have kept the lights burning above the Three Piers of the magical Bridge, none has more clearly and beautifully written thereof than did the great astrologian poet, Isaiah :

"Then the eyes of the blind shall be opened, and the ears of the deaf shall be unstopped. Then shall the lame man leap as a hart, and the tongue of the dumb shall sing; for in the widerness shall waters break out, and streams in the desert. And the glowing sand shall become a pool, and the thirsty ground springs of water; in the habitation of jackals, where they lay, shall be grass with reeds and rushes. And a highway shall be there, and a way and it shall be called, The Way of Holiness; the unclean shall not pass over it, but it shall be for the redeemed; the wayfaring men, yea fools, shall not err therein."

PART THREE

OPTIC THALMUS

The inner eye "the eye behind the eye" just above and attached to the pineal gland by delicate electric wires, is called Optic Thalmus, and means "Light, or Eye of the Chamber."

In the Greek, it means "The Light of the World," "The Candlestick," "Wise Virgins," "The Temple Needs no Light of the Sun," "If Thine Eye be Single, Thy Whole Body shall be Full of Light," and other texts in the New Testament refer to the single eye or Optic Thalmus.

Let us now search for the oil that feeds this wonderful lamp, the All-Seeing Eye.

Christ Jesus is made to say "I am the Light of the World." The word "world" comes from whirl,"to turn as a wheel, to gyrate.

The human body is a certain rate of activity, motion or whirl, i. e. world, and the light of the world and the temple that needs no light of sun or moon refer to the body "Temple of God," when there is "oil in the lamp."

Error is not sanctified by age. It behooves every lover of truth to cast aside prejudice and dogma and find truth.

Until we know the meaning of the words "Jesus" and "Christ" we will not understand the bible, which was written in Greek and Hebrew and translated and retranslated to suit the whims and ignorance of priests and charlatans all down through the centuries. Constantine, a beast in human form, who murdered his mother and boiled his wife in oil, was the chief factor in the orthodox translation of the so-called King James bible.

Constantine was told by the priests of his time that there was no forgiveness of crimes like those that he was guilty of, and so this Roman Emperor devised the plan of salvation, in order that the blood of the innocent Jesus (or Christ) might save him from eternal damnation. An easy way out for this monster, and all the other blood-smeared tyrants, Kings, Emperors and Napoleons of finance, competition and war, from Pharaoh to the present day rulers whose thrones and scepters lie scattered and broken along the Highway of Nations (1917).

"Here the Vassal and the King, side by side, lie withering. Here the sword and scepter rust. "Earth to Earth, and dust to dust."

The word Jesus is from Ichtus, Greek for fish. The word "Christ" means a substance of oil consistency, an ointment or smear. Varnish or paints are used to preserve or save wood or paper or clot—hence they become Saviors.

At about the age of twelve, Jesus was found in the temple arguing with the doctors or teachers. The word "doctor" is from Latin "docere," to teach.

Now read carefully: Every month in the life of every man or woman, when the moon is in the sign that the sun was in at the birth of the individual, there is a psycho-physical seed or "Son of Man" born near the Solar Plexus or the pneumo-gastric plexus which, in the ancient text, was called the "House of Bread," "The Tree of Life," etc. Bethlehem is from Beth, a house, and helm, bread. "Cast thy bread upon the waters and it shall return to thee after many days." Waters are the blood and nerve fluids of the body which carry the fish on its "Divine Journey" to regenerate, save and redeem man. Nazareth means to cook. Nazarene means cooked. Cook means to prepare. Any materialized thing is bread, Nazareth, mass, maso, or dough. Thus the Catholic Mass. Also Maso-n. It will now be made plain why the Masons and Catholics are not in agreement, for our letter N is an abbreviation of the 14th letter of the Hebrew Alphabet, Nun, a fish.

By adding N to Maso, the riddle of cooked or prepared fish was made so plain that the priesthood strenuously objected, and thus developed friction between the church and Masonry.

The disciples were fishermen. The early Christians used a fish as their secret symbol. Money to pay taxes was taken from the mouth of a fish. Bread and fish were increased until 12 baskets full were left, &c. God prepared a fish to swallow Jonah. Jonah means dove. Dove means peace the germ descending from the gray matter of the brain (See baptism of John). The storm means sex desire. The life seed was thus saved. "He that is born of God cannot sin (or fall short of knowledge) for his seed (fish) remaineth in him."—John. The age of puberty is about 12. Up to that age, a child does not understand moral responsibility. "The first born" means the first seed or fish. Pharaoh, sex desire, always tries to destroy the first born. When Jesus was born in Bethlehem, he went (at the age of 12) up the pneumo-gastric nerve, which crosses the medulla oblongata at its junction with the spinal cord at the head of the "River of Jordan," the marrow or nerve fluid of the spinal cord (See illustration in Physiological Charts) and enters the cerebellum, the temple. This is the temple where the moral seed argued with the purely animal cells to change their rate of vibration to moral and spiritual concept. Later this seed (Jesus) drove those who bought and sold ("Even as you and I") with a whip of thongs out of the temple. We must all give up the animal life or suffer the same fate.

Before we explain the baptism in Jordan and the christening and the crucifixion, &c, let us briefly explain Moses, Joshua, Nile, Pharaoh and the children of Israel.

Egypt means the dark lower part of the body. That part of the body below the Solar Plexus is Egypt, or the Kingdom of Earth. All above the center, constitutes the Kingdom of

Heaven. ("The Kingdom of Heaven is within you.") The-Manger, or Bethlehem, is the center, or the balance.

Nile, Moses and Pharaoh's daughter, all refer to generation. (See overflow of Nile). It rises in mountains of the moon. Moses means "drawn from the water." Fish are drawn from water. "There are two fishes in our sea"—Vaughn. See Sign of Pisces, two fishes.

Joshua the Son of Nun. Nun is Hebrew for fish.

Moses was the physical or generative fish. Moses' laws were on the physical plane.

Joshua's laws were spiritual. Joshua means "God of Salvation," and salvation comes from saliva or salivation. Sal is salt which Saves. "If the salt loses its Savor" i. e. Savior, wherewith shall it be salted?" Saliva saves the body by digesting (or preparing) the food. Saliva is a smear or ointment, and so Joshua compares with Christ as Moses compares with Jesus. Moses died on Mt. Nebo. Nebo means understanding. Joshua took the place left vacant by the death of Moses. Jesus was baptized of John in Jordan—the fluids, the Christ substance of the spinal cord, and became, "my beloved Son in whom I am well pleased." There is no J in the Greek or Hebrew alphabets, therefore, the word "John" I O H N meaning "Soul" or "fluids of the body" and not the Ego or Spiritual Man. So when the body dies, the fluids die thus man loses his soul when he loses his body. To prevent the loss of soul and flesh is the mission of the Son, or Seed, of God, or the Son of man.

There are two very small nerves that extend up from Solar Plexus, cross at base of brain and unite at the Optic Thalmus, the eye of the chamber. These nerves, or delicate wires, are called Adi and Pingali. After the seed or fish has been Christed, if it is retained and not wasted in sexual desire, it goes up to "Golgotha," the place of the skull, and crosses the wires, then remains three days in the tomb or the three chambers of the Pineal gland, then it enters the Optic

Thalmus and "giveth light to all that are in the house," that is, the beth or body, all the twelve functions represented by the twelve disciples—the twelve signs of the Zodiac.

But the question will be asked What or where is the source or origin of this seed or redeeming Son? We answer: Ether, Spirit or God. Names mean nothing.

Esse, Universal intelligence, or *It* may be used. *It* breathes into man the breath of life. This elixir is carried through lungs into arteries, or air carriers, where it unites with the inorganic cell-salts, materializes (cooked), and forms granules, and is then deposited as flesh and bone.

The study of Astrology, Biology and Biochemistry, added to Physiology, will lead one into the great Alchemical laboratory of the "Fearfully and wonderfully" made human temple the temple made without sound of saw or hammer.

Before the Neophyte can fully realize the power of the Optic Thalmus, the Divine Eye within his own brain, he must understand the meaning of *Or* especially in its relation to *Word* and *Jordan*.

Iordan (not Jordan) is the word in the original text. I is framed from Iod the 10th letter of the Hebrew Alphabet, and means "hand," or that which creates. Or is gold, not metal, but the "precious substance"—the seed. Dan is Hebrew for Judge, therefore the Creative Power, operating through the precious substance, produces Judgment, or the man of good judgment.

The upper brain is the reservoir of this Or and is the gray matter or "Precious Ointment" of Christ.

"In the beginning was the Word and the Word was God. All things were (or is) created by it," &c.

The upper brain is the Word, and it furnishes all that man contains, or is. Jesus was not a Savior until he was Christed of John in the Jordan. Then he became the "Beloved Son."

Why was the baptism necessary? Because there are two fish. One was Jesus, the Carpenter, the man; the other, the

Christed Jesus the Son of God. The Christ substance gave the electric or magnetic power to the seed to cross the nerves at Golgotha without disintegrating or dying.

To crucify, means to add to or increase a thousand fold. When electric wires are crossed, they set on fire all inflammable substances near them. When the Christed seed crossed the nerve at Golgotha, the veil of the temple was rent and there was an earthquake, and the dead came forth, i. e. the generative cells of the body were quickened or re-generated.

The crucifixion or crossing of the life seed gives power to vibrate the pineal gland at a rate that causes the Optic Thalmus to fill the "whole body with light," and send its vibration out along the optic nerve to the physical eye, and thus heal the blind.

Let us hark back to the Nile : Pharaoh means a ruler or a tyrant or sex desire. Israel means blood, children of Israel, molecules of the blood.

"Moses lifted up the serpent," &c. Moses, the first born, the seed, desired to regenerate the blood and lead it to the promised land, thus he lifted up sex desire, here symboled as the serpent (See the temptation of the Adam and Eve.) ... So shall the "Son of Man be lifted up," &c, &c.—that is put on the cross in order to reach the pineal gland.

"'If I be lifted up, I will draw all men unto me," I will draw all other seed unto me. Study the etymology of "men."

The tree in the midst of the garden bore fruit every month and its leaves were healing.

The Commandment to not eat of the fruit of this tree was not (is not) heeded by the race, and death is the result.

The serpent said "Eat, thou shalt not die," but sex desire was a liar from the beginning.

A noted Professor of Greek, in one of our Universities, says that the translation of many New Testament texts from Greek are radically wrong. For instance, "He that saveth his life, shall lose it, and he that loseth his life, for my sake, shall find it," should read: "He that saveth his seed life shall loosen it (set it free), and he that loosens it, shall find it," which means that this "Bread cast upon the waters" shall redeem him.

Galilee means a circle of water the fluids of the body. Jesus walking on the water is a symbol of the seed, or fish, on its journey. Peter, from petra (stone) is a symbol of physical or material thought which was rescued by the fish, Savior.

The Optic Thalmus is called "The Lamb of God that taketh away the sins of the world"

Sin is from the Hebrew letter Schin, meaning to fall short of knowledge. Sin does not mean wrong or crime, but one may commit a crime or do wrong through lack of knowledge. Paul said:"I die daily" . . . . "I am the chief of sinners." Revelations: "And the lamp thereof is the Lamb." The word, "Lamb," ends with B, which means a house or body of some kind. Now, the optic, or central single eye, is a body, like the outer eye ball; therefore, a beth. This is called lamb by the ancient poet.

Lamp ending with P, which means speech or sending forth or radiating, and is from Pe, the 8th letter of the Hebrew Alphabet, and was used to express light, or knowledge, emanating or going forth from this eye or "Lamb of God."

"As a man thinketh in his heart, so is he."

The cerebellum is heart shaped, and in the Greek is known as the heart. The organ that divides blood was called the "Dividing Pump." The seat of thought is the Cerebellum. Our thoughts shape our lives. If we think continually below the solar plexus in the Kingdom of the Earth; if we dwell in thoughts of material pleasures, we become animal and materialistic. If we really desire the Kingdom of Heaven, we must think of the process that will enable us to realize it.

When Jesus was born, they put him in "swadling clothes." Now the psychic germ (fish) is composed of the concentrated essence of life, and is covered by a gossamer capsule for protection. If this swadling cloth is broken, the "precious ointment" is lost, i. e. it disintegrates and corrupts the blood. In order to save this germ of life, man must remember, that as a man thinketh, so is he. While men must abstain entirely from sexual contact, he must also realize that "He who looketh on a woman to lust after her, hath committed adultery with her in his heart"

By constant prayer do we attain the Kingdom.

Envy, hatred, ambition, covetousness, will destroy the capsule that contains the seed, and thus corrupt the blood as surely as sexual contact. Alcohol in all its deceptive forms is the arch foe to this life-seed, and seeks by every means known to the enemy of man, to destroy it.

"No drunkard shall inherit the Kingdom of Heaven," because alcohol destroys the redeeming substance that enables man to understand or think in his heart the thoughts of the Spirit. Alcohol cuts the capsule that holds the Esse, born every month in Bethlehem. Alcohol eats the fruit of the tree of life.

Gluttony is another enemy to regeneration. All excess of food, all that is not burnt up in the furnace—the stomach and intestinal tract—all that is not properly digested ferments and produces acid which develops alcohol.

Auto intoxication is common among those who overeat. Most everyone overeats.

The furnace, stomach and digestive tract, becomes a distillery, when the surplus food ferments ; and thus becomes Babylon, the home of unclean birds and beasts which pander to carnal mind.

Here we have the reason why sickness was considered Sin by the ancients: "To heal the sick and cast out devils" is the mission of the seed. "He that is born of God cannot sin, or be sick, for his seed remaineth in him." "The blood of Christ cleanseth from all sin"; therefore from all disease.

Here is the physiological explanation : When the Christed substance, the ointment from the river Jordan, the oil in the spinal cord, reaches the pineal gland, it vibrates to a rate that causes new blood the new wine. This is the blood of Christ that heals all infirmities. Unless, so-called, Christians repent of their sins, the doom of the church is at hand; "*Mene, mene teckel upharsin*" is written on the wall.

Here are the words that define a Christian: "These signs shall follow those who believe; they shall lay hands on the sick and they shall recover. They shall cast out devils and raise the dead. All the things that I do, ye shall do, and greater things shall ye do."

If there be one Christian on Earth today, let him stand forth and prove himself worthy. "He that overcometh, I will give to eat of the fruit of the tree of life." To overcome a habit is to cease to do it. When the earthly man is controlled by the spiritual man—the Lord God—he ceases to eat of the fruit, that is, waste it. This fruit is then carried up to the brain and "Eaten in the Father's Kingdom." "And the last enemy to be overcome is death." We overcome death by ceasing to die, and in no other way. "He that believeth in me, shall not perish." Those who die are sinners, and, therefore, are not Christians, for Christ Jesus was (is) without sin. "The wages of Sin is death." "Repent, for sake evil, take up thy Cross, call upon the Lord and He will abundantly pardon." "And the ransomed of the Lord shall return and come to Zion."

When the sexual functions are used for the propagation of human bodies, there is no condemnation or sin. Motherhood is holy, pure, divine. But motherhood forced, is crime. Unwilling motherhood has created the spirit of war and murder and has well nigh destroyed the race. Sexual union for pleasure alone is the broad road that leads to death. "And there shall be no more *Curse*"—Revelation. The word "Curse" has no reference to an oath. Curse means friction, to grind. The statement, "Then Peter began to curse and

swear" ... And immediately the cock crew," when understood physiologically, fully explains the meaning of curse.
Sexual commerce for the birth of children where the parents
sacrifice themselves for their offsprings' sake, or total abstinence, is written with a pen of flame on all the pages of ancient Scriptures and modern biology.

"And I saw a woman clothed with the Sun, having the
Moon under her feet and twelve stars upon her head." The
Sun is the "Son of Man," the product of her own body saved
and lifted up. The Moon refers to the generative life. Twelve
stars are the twelve functions, typified by twelve zodiacal
signs, which she has mastered through physical regeneration.

Miss Ruth Le Prade, the woman poet of the New Time,
sings of the Kingdom as follows :

"I am a woman free. My song
Flows from my soul with pure and joyful strength.
It shall be heard through all the noise of things—
A song of joy where songs of joy were not.
My sister singers, singing in the past,
Sang songs of melody but not of joy—
For woman's name was Sorrow, and the slave
Is never joyful, tho he smiles.

"I am a woman free. Too long
I was held captive in the dust. Too long
My soul was surfeited with toil or ease
And rotted as the plaything of a slave.
I am a woman free at last
After the crumbling centuries of time.
Free to achieve and understand;
Free to become and live.

I am a woman free. With face
Turned toward the sun, I am advancing
Toward love that is not lust,
Toward work that is not pain,
Toward home which is the world,
Toward motherhood which is not forced,
And toward the man who also must be free.

With face turned toward the sun,
Strong and radiant-limbed,
I advance, singing,
And my song is as free
As the soul from which it flows.
I advance toward that which is, but was not;
I, the free woman, advance singing,
And with face turned toward the sun.
Let Ignorance and Tyranny
Tremble at the sound of my feet.

"When thou prayest, enter into thy closet and pray to thy Father in secret, and he shall reward thee openly." The word Secret is derived from Secretions. The upper brain, the Cerebrum, contains the secretions, gray matter, creative, or that creates, builds and supplies all life-force of the human temple.—Soul of Man's (Solomon's temple). Hence God, the Creator, dwells in you. The cerebrum is his throne.

Prayer or desires expressed by man in the cerebellum for righteousness, is answered in the cerebrum. Thus by prayer to God within, and in no other way, can man overcome the adversary or the "carnal mind which is at enmity to God."

Let us now consider the Virgin Mary.

Virgin, pure. Mar-y, or mare, water. Virgin Mary, pure water. Pure Sea. Pure Ether or spirit.

Fish come out of the water. The water, or fluids, of the body give birth to the seed, or fish.

The Virgin Mary is not mentioned in the Allegory after the ascension of the Christed Jesus the redeemed fish. Each person, male or female, must "work out their own salvation" All so-called sex reform, that tolerates union of sexes, may be answered by :

"There is a way that
Seemeth right to man
The end of which is death."
"In my Kingdom there is no marrying nor
          giving in marriage,
But they are as the
Angels in Heaven."

Eden, good dwelling place, and Promised Land, mean the same. The children, molecules, of Israel, blood, crossed the Jordan in order to reach Eden.

Jordan is the spinal cord, and the pneumo-gastric nerve crosses, at the junction of this cord, with the body known as Medulla oblongata, and thus connects with the cerebellum, which is the anteroom or Eden—the head—the "Thalmus" or chamber that contains the "Single Eye," the pineal gland and upper brain or cerebellum.

Eden's garden is the human body.

The solar (center) plexus, with the pneumogastric plexus and its branches, is the "Tree of Life." The pneumo-gastric nerve is also called vagus nerve, because its branches wander. Vagrant, wandering, is from vagus, to wander.

"A river went out of Eden to water the garden, and from thence it was parted and became four heads. The name of the first is Pishon; the second, Gihon; the third, Hiddekel; the fourth, Euphrates. The river is saliva. Pishon is the urine; Gihon is the intestinal tract; Hiddekel is the blood; Euphrates the nerve fluids, especially the creative.

Abram and Sara, or Sarai, had the letter H added to their names when the angel appeared to them and gave instructions. See Gen. 16, 17 and 18. H is from Heth, the eighth letter of the Hebrew alphabet, and means a field or a vision. The meaning of Heath (H) is given in the Jewish Kaballa and Tarot card symbols as "Spiritual Perception"—field, or vision.

Sarah gave birth to Isaac after this regeneration. Isaac means laughter, a symbol of happiness; so the story is a symbol of physical regeneration.

The story of Job is evidently a fable. The letters I. O. B. (No J in Hebrew alphabet) figures up, numerically, 19, which means "resplendent light."

Regeneration develops the optic thalmus, or single eye, by furnishing the oil necessary to light the chamber or Eden. "And the temple needs no light of Sun, Moon or Stars," &c.

Job, on the generative plane, his experience in the Kingdom of Earth, suffered great trials, tribulations and disease; and while he argued much about God and kept his faith, he failed to comprehend.

But after he became regenerated, he exclaimed: "I have heard of thee by the hearing of the ear, but now mine eye seeth thee." Notice mine eye, not eyes.

So here we have another proof that regeneration opens the Optic Thalmus—the eye behind the eyes.

And now in closing: No page of the wonders of the human body—the temple of the living God—is more divinely scientific than the parable that follows:

"The foolish man built his house on the sand
And the rain washed it away."
"The wise man built his house on a rock
And it stood the storms, for it was builded upon
        a rock."

The Bible is a compilation of astronomical, physiological and anatomical symbols, allegories and parables.

In the technical terms of modern chemistry and physiology, the above text is explained as follows : Sand and cement form rock or stone. Sand alone, without some medium cement is unstable, simply "shifting sand."

The Pineal gland, the dynamo that runs the organism of man, is composed of sand plus a cement, an ointment, a smear, found, as has been explained, in large quantity in the spinal cord, also, to some extent, in all parts of the body. When this cement is wasted, as the Prodigal Son wasted his substance in riotous living, there being a deficiency of this precious oil, the pineal gland becomes brittle, and does not vibrate at a rate that vitalizes the blood and tissue at the health and strength rate, and the house, beth or body, falls.

In the common slang of the hour, we say: "He lacks the sand" or "grit."

The mineral salts of blood were called sand or salt by Hebrews. The cell-salts that are found in the pineal gland are chiefly potassium phosphate, the base of the gray matter of the brain; but all of the 12 inorganic salts are represented. In Revelations, the pineal gland is called "The white stone" In Biochemistry, the phosphate of potassium is given as the birth-salts of Aries people.

Those who build their house upon a rock are they who conserve the substance that unites with the sand—cell-salts—and thus forms the rock upon which a body may be built that will be free from sin and sickness.

The mission of Jesus, the Christ, was to triumph over death and the grave, over matter, and transmute his body, and be able, also, to materialize at will. He not only succeeded in doing this, but stated most emphatically that all the things that he did, we may do also.

> Did he proclaim the truth?
> Answer thou of little faith!
> "Rock of Ages cleft for me,

Let me hide myself in thee."

And the Christ Substance shall create the cement that completes the rock surface of the bridge that crosses the three-span gulf between the shores of conception and birth. Thus "Shall Mortal put on immortality" and the last enemy, death, shall be overcome."

A VISION OF IMMORTALITY

It seemed to me that it was noon of a perfect day, and that I was wide awake. I stood upon a mountain top in Southern California and looked out to the West. I saw the clean page of the Balboa Sea.

Catalina Island reflected its hills and crags in the curling mists that rose and twisted about like things alive, and the mirage grew and spread until I fancied that the new Jerusalem was descending out of the Heavens.

Eastward the Sierra Madre peaks lightly veiled their heads with mist and fleecy clouds, as if to gently subdue their ineffable glory. I saw the clean-trunked eucalypti, the pendant pepper boughs and the orange groves. A shuttle-throated mocking bird was pouring liquid melody into the ears of Deity, and I asked aloud, "Is not this immortality? Am I not immortal?"

And then a voice, sweet as the voice of the Infinite Mother, came out of the everywhere, and I heard the words, "Yes! you are immortal. You stood in the rush of Divine Splendor when God said: 'Let there be light.' You heard the morning stars chant the Epic of Creation. You saw the first procession of the Constellations. You saw Orion light his clustering lamp out in the wilderness of the southern skies. You saw Arcturus rise from the unknown sea of silence, and sentinel the Northern Pole. You saw the first rushing, blazing Comet emerge from the awful realms of boundless space, sweep across measureless reaches of star-dust, bearing upon its flaming front the glad intelligence that the rule of law is perfect; that Suns, Stars, Systems obey the Cosmic urge and obey the Eternal Word. And, if in the operation of wisdom, the time shall come when the vast fabric of creation shall rock in universal spasm and totter to its fall, if the elements shall melt in fervent heat, the last Sun die and the 'Heavens be gathered together as a scroll,' yet thou, oh doubting one, shall stand erect, unafraid and

> 'O'er the ruins smile
> And light thy torch again
> At Nature's funeral pile.'

Then I heard the bugles all sing truce along the iron front of war. I saw the battle flags furled. Soldiers were transformed into men. They returned to homes, shops, the fields, the orchards and gardens. Children laughed and women loved. The headsman and hangman retired and became forgotten horrors. Grass grew over the battle trenches, flowers bloomed over deserted forts, vines clambered over arsenals and dreadnaughts rusted in the harbors. Earth was baptized with the golden light of love.

With the "Eye behind the eyes," "I saw the Holy City beside the tideless Sea" and I heard the Angels striking all their harps of gold.

END.